Ernest Race

HAZEL CONWAY

For Zara

Ernest Race

First edition published in the United Kingdom
1982 by The Design Council, 28 Haymarket
London SW1Y 4SU

Printed and bound in the United Kingdom by
The Whitefriars Press Limited

© Hazel Conway 1982

British Library CIP Data

Conway, Hazel
  Ernest Race.
  1. Race, Ernest
  I. Title
  749.22   NK2542.R/

ISBN 0-85072-128-8

THE
DESIGN
COUNCIL

Contents

SALLY RACE/SANDRA FLETT

Ernest Race FSIAD, RDI, 1913–64.

Introduction

Ernest Race's career as a professional furniture designer dates from the end of the Second World War, when the only furniture that was allowed to be made in this country was Utility; there were severe shortages of materials for furniture-making and it hardly seemed a propitious moment to launch a new career. Race had been involved in design before the war, but his main concern then had been with textiles. In the 1930s, when he trained as a designer and started his career, the main influence on architecture and design was the International Modern Movement. The work of Le Corbusier, Mies van der Rohe and Gropius was becoming better known among architects and designers in Britain, though it was by no means widely accepted here; indeed, both traditional and revivalist architects and designers were loud in their criticisms. Race's career as a designer thus spanned the 1930s, the period of Utility furniture, the flourishing of 'contemporary' design in the 1950s, and continued into the early 1960s. In 1964 he died at the early age of 49.

The study of the work of a furniture designer involves much more than an evaluation of his particular work, for furniture design – like all other design – cannot be looked at in isolation from the context in which it was produced and used. Although books or museums may show a particular item of furniture in isolation, in real life it appears with other furniture in rooms. Whether the room be a sitting room, dining room or office, the furniture can be arranged in a variety of ways. Every period has its own ways of arranging furniture and the post-war period is no exception. The importance of this to the study of furniture design lies in the information it can provide about the use of furniture in a range of contexts. These uses in turn form part of the influences on the design and on the designer.

The interior design of a room includes the curtains, carpets, wallcoverings, lighting and furniture. In the period immediately post 1945 one of the main factors influencing the design of domestic interiors was a shortage of space. As a result of bombing, housing shortages were severe and the main emphasis initially was on building council houses. These tended to have smaller rooms than the equivalent housing that was built in the 1930s. Shortage of space also showed itself in the private sector, for as no new houses for the private market were being built, there was increasing pressure, with people returning from the war, on the stock that was available.

This shortage of space manifested itself in several ways that had a direct influence on furniture design. For example, the development of multi-purpose rooms such as the dining/sitting room meant that furniture had to be adaptable to both uses, rather than being designed solely for the dining room or the sitting room. For multi-purpose rooms the furniture needed to be lighter, so that it could be moved easily to suit the various purposes. Room dividers, often in the form of free-standing open shelves of varying height, were introduced; these divided the space visually into different areas for different functions. Painting the walls different shades was another method of achieving an apparent division of space. Another development that helped to create a sense of space in cramped conditions was that of unit furniture that fitted together and combined the functions of sideboard, storage cabinet and bookshelves. The bulkiest items in the sitting room were the upholstered pieces. If this bulk could be reduced then the feeling of space would be enhanced without comfort being sacrificed. Race's work in this area was most important. Other developments that had a significant influence on the layout of the sitting room in this period were central heating and the television set; both had the effect of taking the focus of the room away from the fireplace.

Because everyone has experience of their own furniture in their own home the tendency is to think of furniture primarily in that context. But on looking around one realises that furniture appears in practically every environment that one can think of: aeroplanes, offices, schools, stations, parks, all have furniture. The furniture industry divides its output into two main categories, domestic furniture and contract furniture. Contract furniture is usually manufactured in considerable quantities for such public, semi-public and commercial uses as hospitals, schools, shops and offices. Race's work as a furniture designer covered both the domestic and the contract areas.

Another area which a study of furniture design cannot ignore is that of architecture. Architecture and building provide the spatial environment for furniture, and in many periods the theories influencing architecture and design have a common source. This was particularly true of the period 1945 to around 1965, when the predominant influences on the criteria applied to architecture and design in England were those of the Modern Movement. This study seeks to examine Race's contribution to design in the context of the periods in which he was working and to ask what were the most important factors influencing the forms that his designs took. This approach implies that unless aesthetics and style were the most important factors influencing the final design, they will not be emphasised. The approach to design history that gives predominance to style and form is very limited, and can come between a design and attempts to understand it, obscuring rather than clarifying what were the most important issues in the evolution of a particular design.

The limitations imposed by the size of this book have meant that the main emphasis must be on Race's designs. A fuller contextual study that relates these to the designs of his contemporaries at home and abroad and to a more detailed study of the architecture and interior design of the period, must wait for another occasion. That Race's contribution to furniture design was significant is not in doubt. He was awarded the Gold Medal and the Silver Medal for two of his chairs at the Tenth Milan Triennale in 1954. He received three Design Centre Awards and a Gold Medal at the California State Exhibition in 1962, and he gained in 1953 the highest professional distinction available to a designer in this country: the appointment to the Royal Society of Arts' Faculty of Royal Designers for Industry, which is limited to 40 members.

His own professional organisation, the Society of Industrial Artists (SIA, now the Society of Industrial Artists and Designers, SIAD), recognised his design abilities early in his career, electing him a Fellow in 1947. In 1958/9 he was elected President and in 1963 shortly before his death early the following year he was awarded the Society's Annual Medal.

Some designers leave a wealth of material behind them in the form of drawings, letters and a variety of other documents. The task of the historian is then to assess the work of the designer, not only in terms of the projects he produced but also from such archival sources. However, the case of Race is very different, for he did not leave a wealth of documentation behind. Such working drawings as are still extant were drawn by others and date in most instances from several years after the project was put into production. Although Race did write occasional articles for publication, they were few, and evidence of correspondence is very sparse. Fortunately there are many people still alive who worked with Race and knew him professionally and it is from them that much of the information for this book is drawn. All agreed that Race was a sincere and modest man whose quiet sense of humour is perhaps indicated in this drawing of him with his car.

Race and his De Dion Bouton, whose roof was by no means watertight. The sight of him drawing up to the factory in his car with his umbrella up was not uncommon!

Ernest Race and Ernest Race Ltd

Ernest Race was born in Newcastle upon Tyne in 1913. His early training and design experience gave little indication that his major contribution would be in the area of furniture design, for he trained as an interior designer and his main design interests until 1939 were in textiles.

After leaving St Paul's School, London, in 1932, Race went to the Bartlett School of Architecture, where he took a three-year certificate course in interior design. His future wife Sally was also taking this course. Like many architectural schools in this country, the Bartlett School was at that time rather old fashioned, unaffected by modern educational developments and virtually unaware of the existence of the Modern Movement.[1] After working for a brief period with a model-maker, Race joined the lighting firm Troughton and Young as a draughtsman. This company was very forward looking and was making Bauhaus-type light fittings as early as 1934[2] (Fig 1).

In 1937 Race went out to India for four months to stay with his rather eccentric and very forceful missionary aunt Blanche Tweddle, who ran a weaving village near Madras called Ikadu Village Industries. Miss Tweddle had been involved in this project for many years, and Race had grown up with their fabrics in his home. The quality of the material was excellent. While with his aunt, Race did some designs based on the traditional weaving patterns, and on his return to London opened a shop in Motcomb Street to sell the fabrics (Figs 2 and 3). Race had many young architect friends and thus was able to build up the contract side of the business as well as make a success of the retail side.[3] Indian cotton at this time was subject to Imperial preference and because there was practically no duty on it, it could be sold at very competitive prices. Furthermore, the abstract designs of Race's fabrics seemed appropriate for a variety of interiors, including those of Modern Movement architects. Among the architects who used these fabrics were Maxwell Fry, F.R.S. Yorke and Walter Gropius. Race fabrics were used at Impington Village College (Walter Gropius and Maxwell Fry, 1937–9), one of the village colleges evolved from the ideas of Henry Morris, Education Secretary of Cambridgeshire[4] (Fig 4).

SILVER COLLECTION, MIDDLESEX POLYTECHNIC

Fig 1: Ultralux light, A. B. Read, c1934 (Troughton & Young).

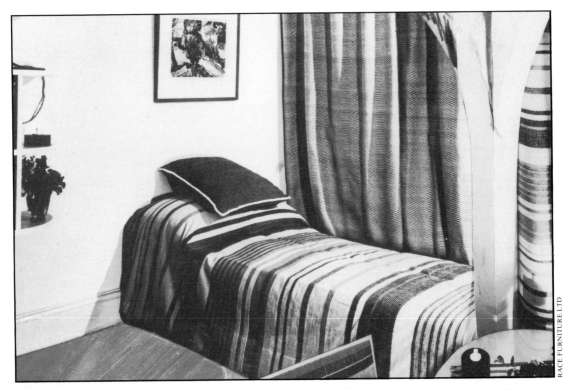

RACE FURNITURE LTD

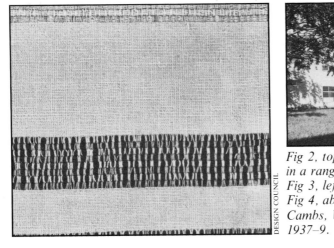

DESIGN COUNCIL

BRITISH ARCHITECTURAL LIBRARY/RIBA

Fig 2, top: Race fabric sold at Motcomb Street in a range of colours and varied surface textures.
Fig 3, left: Detail of a Race fabric.
Fig 4, above: Impington Village College, Cambs, Walter Gropius and Maxwell Fry, 1937–9.

In his Motcomb Street shop Race had chairs by Gerald Summers of The Makers of Simple Furniture (Fig 5), a further indication that he was in touch with modern developments in architecture and design. His handwoven fabrics, clear in design and colour, provided a warm contrast with such modern interiors as those at Impington; the fabrics themselves were not avant-garde nor ever thought to be so either by Race or by those using them,[5] though certain common qualities can be seen between them and some of the textiles produced at the Bauhaus in the late 1920s (Fig 6).

Looking back on this period, Race recalled that in the dreary world of furniture the only bright spots were the forward-looking firms of Gordon Russell and Heal's, and occasional glimpses of work from Sweden and Finland.

'As a design student in England in the mid-1930s one was all too conscious of the depths to which the British domestic arts had sunk . . . It was to Scandinavia that we turned for a breath of fresh air . . . Sweden seemed to be the centre of progressive modern design; one heard less of Danish and Finnish work, with the exception of Alvar Aalto's exciting chairs in laminated wood.'[6] (Figs 7 and 8).

Both Gordon Russell and Heal's were exceptional in giving opportunities to young designers, whereas in the rest of the trade there was virtually nothing.[7] A freelance furniture designer in Britain tended, with a few exceptions, to have to peddle sketches of sideboards and wardrobes round High Wycombe and the East End of London, which were the main centres of the furniture industry, for as little as three for 7/6d (37½p). Race recalled hearing of someone who applied for a job as designer at a large factory and was asked how long it would take him to design a sideboard. The applicant thought it might take

VICTORIA & ALBERT MUSEUM

Fig 5: Plywood chair, Gerald Summers, 1934.

THE BAUHAUS BY H. M. WINGLER

Fig 6: Wool fabrics, Lis Beyer, c1926 (Bauhaus).

him about a week and he was told that that was no use at all, the last chap had turned out six designs a day![8]

In 1938 Race began training part-time as a fireman with the Auxiliary Fire Service. The following year the Motcomb Street shop was closed down when he was called up into the A.F.S. where he remained for the duration of the war. During the war his design activities did not stop completely, as he designed some unit furniture that was made up for him by firemen.[9] When the war ended he joined the architects Colcutt and Hamp for a short time to make models, while continuing to design unit furniture at home. It was the design of this unit furniture[10] that was one of the factors that led in 1945 to the partnership of Noel Jordan and

Fig 7, below: Long chair, Alvar Aalto, 1937 (Artek).
Fig 8, opposite: 'Eva' easy chair, Bruno Mathsson, 1934 (Karl Mathsson).

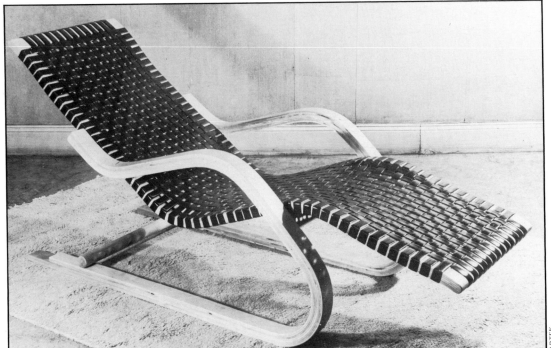

ARTEK

Ernest Race, to the formation of Ernest Race Ltd, and to the beginning of Race's career as a professional furniture designer.

J.W. Noel Jordan (1907–74) qualified as an engineer, worked in the Development Department of The Dunlop Rubber Co Ltd, and subsequently set up his own light engineering company, Enness Sentinel Ltd, in Clapham, London in 1939. During the war the company manufactured gas converters, which replaced petrol engines in buses, cars and fire engines; ships' davits for lifeboats; and certain parts for the Mulberry Harbour. As the end of the war approached, Noel Jordan recognised that he would have to develop a new area of production suitable for peace-time and decided on that of furniture. Looking back on this

DESIGN COUNCIL

decision he wrote: 'I did realise I knew nothing about furniture design, or for that matter, furniture; but I had a strong feeling that engineering methods of construction would probably be economic and an improvement on existing methods.'[11]

Noel Jordan advertised in *The Times* for a furniture designer and received more than 300 replies, among them one from Ernest Race. On receipt of Race's application Noel Jordan wrote briefly to him setting out his ideas on furniture design and manufacture in the context of the shortage of hardwoods, which was likely to continue for some considerable time. 'The demand for furniture, particularly that of first class artistic merit, will be tremendous. It therefore follows that an original designer, prepared to utilise new materials, such as steel, plywood, plastics (not necessarily the moulded type), aluminium, together with new methods of finish of such materials, is presented with a unique opportunity for developing his work.'[12]

What sort of design was Noel Jordan thinking of at this time? 'The work . . . must be creative, not merely copies of old masters, or cubist, but durable, functional and of appeal.'[13] The sort of production run that he was thinking of would be in the order of 100 or so articles of each design, in other words not mass production, and the designer would be responsible for the selection of materials, though assistance in this would be available. The designer would also have a free hand in naming his work, and the company would be opening showrooms in London to display its products, and would advertise in first-class journals.

After a series of meetings Noel Jordan and Ernest Race agreed to form a new company, Ernest Race Ltd, with Noel Jordan as Managing Director and Race as Director and Chief Designer.[14] Race would be responsible for all designs manufactured by the company and no design would be manufactured unless Race approved it. Noel Jordan felt it would be an advantage to call the company Ernest Race Ltd because of Race's pre-war connections with architects and designers, and he also felt there were certain advantages in using a personal title (Fig 9).[15]

Noel Jordan was correct in recognising that the demand for furniture would increase, for the Board of Trade was at this time looking at ways of expanding the range of furniture designs that could be approved and accepted as 'Utility', that is of reaching an approved standard.

Fig 9: Ernest Race Ltd catalogue, 1947. Front cover featuring the company logo of a horse.

RACE

FURNITURE

The Utility Furniture Scheme

The development of Utility design was precipitated by the outbreak of the Second World War (3 September 1939) and the shortages of material that resulted from the dramatic decrease in imported goods. Foodstuffs and petrol were imported and rationing was introduced; timber was in extremely short supply and between July 1940 and February 1941 no timber at all was available for civilian furniture. For those who were trying to control civilian consumption and regulate industrial production, furniture presented a particular problem, for while in terms of the war effort it had a low priority, it was needed for the services, for homes destroyed by bombing and for those setting up home for the first time. The problem was to see that what little there was, was fairly distributed. Furniture could not be rationed so that everyone got one table, one bed, and one chair a year, so the solution was allocation; that is to say, you were entitled to buy it if you could prove your need.

Prices could be controlled, as prices of other goods were controlled, but how could the quality of furniture be assured? A chair's price could be fixed at, say, £2 but this did not ensure £2 worth of value. The solution proposed was a standard design that could be easily checked, was simple enough to avoid wastage of raw materials and labour, and of a sufficiently high quality to give a long and useful life. This was the origin of Utility furniture.[1]

The key figures in the Utility scheme were Hugh Dalton, President of the Board of Trade 1942–5, and Gordon Russell, head of the Utility furniture design team. Of all the wartime Utility schemes, that for furniture was an unparalleled example of total state control, not only of the supply, but also of the design, and it was the magnitude of the problem of rationing the almost non-existent supplies of timber that led to the application of such a drastic measure. No other items were controlled in the same way, with the exception of pencils, radio receivers and cigarette lighters, which were all related to the use of wood. Matches were in short supply, for example, so a Utility lighter was devised. Other Utility goods such as clothing and pottery were limited in the amount of material and labour that could be used in their manufacture, but the designs were not specified.

The design brief for the first Utility furniture was that it should be strong and serviceable, only hardwoods such as oak and mahogany were to be used for the main structure, and all joints were to be strongly mortised or pegged. Because plywood was unobtainable in the early years of the war, panels of veneered hardboard were specified. Several designs were submitted to the Advisory Committee on Utility Furniture and those of Clinch and Cutler selected (Fig 10).

BOARD OF TRADE

Fig 10: Chiltern Utility tallboy, light oak, model no 5, 1943, E. Clinch and H. T. Cutler.

Most of the cabinets stood on plinths rather than legs; the wood sections were thin, but the panels of the doors were subdivided to make them strong despite the thin sections used. The framed and panelled doors gave this furniture a somewhat period look. The knobs and handles were of wood as plastics were needed for the war effort, but despite the steel shortage screws were used which added strength to the furniture. This furniture was called the Chiltern range and after 28 February 1943 no furniture other than Utility could be sold (Figs 11 and 12). Utility furniture was exempt from Purchase Tax in order to keep prices as low as possible, was available by permit to newly-weds and bombed families, and was intended to cover basic necessities.

It was Gordon Russell who felt that once the first Utility designs had been produced matters should not be allowed to rest there. With research into design the Utility specification could be used as the basis of a quality mark for furniture in the post-war period. He suggested that a panel should study this and as a result he was asked to become chairman of the Design Panel that was set up in June 1943. By April 1945 the end of the war in Europe was in sight, so furniture supplies would need to be increased and greater variety in the range of furniture available seemed desirable. Gordon Russell's panel had been working with this problem in mind, and in March 1946 the Board of Trade held an exhibition of 50 pieces of prototype Utility furniture, the first real changes in the scheme since it had been introduced. The existing Chiltern range was shown, together with some additions that had been made to it since its introduction; a completely new range, the Cotswold; and a range called initially Cockaigne, then Cheviot, which never went into production (Figs 13 and 14).

The Cotswold range developed by the Design Panel made a much greater use of blockboard and plywood than the Chiltern had, and it was characterised by an extensive use of flush panels and veneers; consequently it was not only physically lighter, but it also appeared lighter. The Cotswold was put into production in 1946.

'. . . There wasn't enough timber for bulbous legs or enough labour for even the cheapest carving, and straightforward commonsense lines were efficient and economical . . . it must have been a bit of a shock that a type of design which had been pioneered for years by a small minority – whilst the trade looked on and laughed – should prove its mettle in a national emergency but so it was, to the amusement of some and the amazement of others.'[2]

Assessments of the impact of Utility furniture on furniture design in the post-war period vary. One view was that its simplicity – so different from the more traditional design of the 1930s – was directly in line with the Bauhaus and machine aesthetic ideas of functional simplicity (see page 21). It was also argued that the 'acceptance' by the public of Utility furniture paved the way for a more simple style of design after the war. However, the facts do not entirely bear out this view. For one thing, Utility was the only new furniture available, so its 'acceptance' by the public is very debatable for they had no other choice. Furthermore, a superficial glance at 'contemporary' design in the 1950s (see page 36) hardly indicated that it was simple style.

It is in the area of the experience of the manufacturers that produced Utility furniture that the impact of Utility furniture seems more significant. The Board of Trade Utility designs achieved a standard of design, in terms of construction, joining, use of materials and simple forms, that compared well with the best pre-war work and indeed was in advance of the general level of pre-war design in this country. Those furniture manufacturers that continued

BOARD OF TRADE

BOARD OF TRADE

manufacturing furniture during the war learnt from the ideas behind Utility while those who changed from furniture production to war production also learnt new ways of handling wood and the potential of new materials such as synthetic resin adhesives. In the immediate post-war period the shortage of wood stimulated experimental work by furniture and other manufacturers in alternative materials, particularly with plastics and light alloys.

As peace came the need for extreme economy

MANOR STUDIO

DESIGN COUNCIL

Fig 11, top: Chiltern tallboy, oak, model no 304, 1947. These later versions had metal handles.
Fig 12, above: Chiltern settee, 1947.
Fig 13, above right: Daily Herald Modern Homes Exhibition, 1946. From left: Cockaigne chest of drawers, Cotswold cupboard and chest of drawers.
Fig 14, right: Ideal Home Exhibition, 1948. Cotswold dressing table and stool.

of resources passed (even though these resources – particularly wood for furniture making – were not in anything like good supply), and the Board of Trade came under pressure from both manufacturers and consumers to include a wider range of goods in the Utility scheme. This would avoid giving advantages through preferential taxation to some goods and some manufacturers rather than to others. Among the recommendations made by the Board of Trade were that metal firms and the plastics industry be allowed to make furniture, provided their designs were approved as being within the Utility scheme; that wicker furniture should be introduced; that factory zoning should be abandoned; and that furniture could be imported provided this did not affect the quotas for imported timber. While supplies of furniture lagged behind demand, the Board of Trade recommended that price control should continue to be linked to approved specifications and designs, and that items qualifying for the

Furniture selected by the Council of Industrial Design as typical of what occurred after the lifting of the Utility design restrictions in 1948.

Fig 15: 'It will be noticed that the pre-war vogue for "reproduction" furniture has been resuscitated by manufacturers. Whether or not the simpler lines of the utility range have given the public a taste for something more in keeping with contemporary life remains to be seen.' (CoID caption, 1949).

Fig 16: 'We were told so often that life was drab, but a very large number of people preferred the simplicity of utility furniture, with its sound standards of construction, to these attempts at "glamour", where quality of workmanship was sacrificed in an attempt to achieve surface appeal.' (CoID caption, 1950).

Utility label should be expanded.[3]

It was not until 1948 that the Board of Trade ended the requirement that Utility furniture be made to approved designs, and even then two main restrictions remained. The label 'Utility furniture' was limited to a number of basic pieces that included a bookcase, but not a china cabinet or gramophone record cabinet, and minimum dimensions for each type of article and many component parts were laid down. For each piece of furniture a maximum price was set for items that could be sold tax free; for example, a 2ft (61cm) wardrobe had to cost £12 or less to qualify for being tax free, a 4ft (122cm) wardrobe £25 or less.[4] Non-Utility furniture at this time (1948) was subject to Purchase Tax of $66\frac{2}{3}$ per cent, which was later reduced to $33\frac{1}{3}$ per cent. It was thus very much to a manufacturer's advantage to see that his furniture qualified as Utility, and much ingenuity was involved in doing so (Figs 15 and 16). During the three-month period from April to June 1951, the proportion of Utility production to total home suppliers of furniture was over 90 per cent,[5] and it was not until 21 January 1953 that the Utility Furniture Scheme, together with the quality control associated with it, was finally ended.

The new company of Ernest Race Ltd was set

Living room with dining recess

RACE FURNITURE LTD

Fig 17: Aluminium alloy and Holoplast furniture shown in Ernest Race Ltd catalogue, 1947.

up while the Board of Trade was looking for new ways in which to expand the range of furniture designs that would be approved as Utility, and it needed a licence from the Board of Trade to make furniture. This was duly obtained from the Director of Furniture Production, and it allowed the company to make unlimited quantities of furniture provided that no licensed material was used in the contruction (these licensed materials included all types of hardwood). The materials that were available were those associated with aircraft production, chiefly aluminium in sheet or ingot form, and also steel rod. The unit furniture that Race had designed at the end of the war had influenced Noel Jordan's decision to form a partnership with him, but this furniture was made of wood. In the first few months of the company's life both partners spent considerable time and money trying to evolve a form of unit furniture that could be made from aluminium sheeting, with the result that the company ran quite short of capital.

While trying to solve this problem, Race had been involved in designing dining chairs, tables and a sideboard/cabinet from precast aluminium and Holoplast (a honeycomb section of plastic with a thin veneer of mahogany, Fig 17). It was this range – particularly the dining chair BA 3 (Fig 18) – that restored the company's financial situation and brought it to the attention of important retailers such as Heal's and Dunn's. In 1954 the BA 3 chair was awarded a Gold Medal at the Milan Triennale, and between 1945 and 1969 more than 250,000 were produced. Even as late as 1963 the company was receiving requests for these chairs to be re-covered or mended.[6]

'(We) have a set of Race armchairs Reg. Des. No. 848794 in our ladies' shoe department . . . purchased 24 years ago . . . ' The letter continued that the shop had recently suffered considerable damage, the BA chairs had been buried under rubble and the arm of one chair was broken, and asked if the company still had replacements.[7]

DESIGN COUNCIL

Fig 18: The BA 3 cast aluminium alloy dining chair, 1946 (designed 1945).

The BA Chair and Metal Furniture

To today's eyes everything about the BA chair (Fig 19) appears strange: the forms, the materials, even the colours. It is of cast aluminium alloy and thus qualifies as metal furniture, but it shares none of the characteristics of the metal furniture that became familiar in the years before 1939. The light cantilevered designs of Breuer, Stam and others (Figs 20, 21 and 22) had introduced a completely new conception of metal furniture which exploited the strength and springiness of tubular steel.

Aluminium alloy is much lighter than steel[1] and, although its strength is comparable to that of mild steel, it can, depending on specification, bend much more under loads. The aluminium alloy furniture produced in the 1930s used the material in sheet and bar form to produce designs that were not only light in weight because of the material used, but also light in appearance because of the forms of the design and the finish of the aluminium alloy. Marcel Breuer's aluminium chair (Fig 23) relates to the forms he used in plywood (Fig 24), but utilises the particular mechanical properties of aluminium alloy. He used two flat bars of alloy, each cut along their centre lines almost to the end. One of these strips supported the seat and formed the back, the other formed the armrest. In the Landi Stuhl by H. Coray (Fig 25) one sheet of pressed alloy formed the seat and body of the chair, which was supported on a frame of solid bar-section alloy. In both chairs the finish of the material as well as the form added much to the feeling of lightness. They thus showed some of the 'machine aesthetic' characteristics so sought after by the European avant-garde in the inter-war period.

The machine aesthetic was concerned not only with visual qualities, but also with the whole question of the search for an architecture and design appropriate to the twentieth century (the *Zeitgeist*) and the identification of particular factors that distinguished the twentieth century from all previous centuries. It was concerned with the design of machine-produced goods and with the social, economic and political implications of mass production. It was also concerned with the imagery associated with machine production: materials should be so formed that the resulting products appeared as if they had been made by machine, even though they had in fact been made by 'hand'. The machine aesthetic was particularly concerned with new machinery in the area of transport, for transport was identified as one of the chief distinguishing features of this century. It was also concerned with the 'idea' and the 'ideal' of the machine in general rather than specific terms. Among the main contributors to the development of the machine aesthetic were the de Stijl group founded by Theo van Doesburg in Holland in 1917, the Constructivists in Russia around 1921, the Purists founded by Ozenfant and Jeanneret (Le Corbusier) in 1918, and Le Corbusier's book *Vers une Architecture* first published in 1923.[2]

The machine aesthetic was most important because it influenced the criteria applied to design by the Modern Movement. These criteria persisted virtually unchallenged in the post-war period in England, until the advent of pop design in the late 1950s and early 1960s.

In the Modern Movement simple surface finishes and geometric forms were seen as the forms most appropriate for machine production. These forms became identified with, and symbolised 'functional' design and no matter how function was determined, ornamentation and decoration were eschewed. The terms 'modern' design – meaning simple, basically geometric forms – and 'functional' design became virtually interchangeable in the Modern Movement and both implied 'good'

Fig 19, below: BA 3 chair, Ernest Race, 1946.
Fig 20, bottom: Cesca chair, Marcel Breuer, 1928.
Fig 21, right: S33 chair, Mart Stam, 1926.
Fig 22, below right: M22 chair, 1936 (Cox & Co).

DESIGN COUNCIL ARCHIVE

VICTORIA & ALBERT MUSEUM

ARAM DESIGNS LTD

DESIGN COUNCIL COLLECTION SHERIDAN COAKLEY

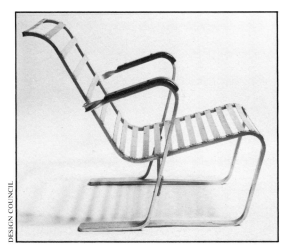

DESIGN COUNCIL

Fig 23, left: Aluminium alloy chair, Marcel Breuer, 1933.
Fig 24, below left: Laminated birch long chair, Marcel Breuer, 1936 (Isokon).
Fig 25, below: Aluminium alloy Landi chair, H. Coray, 1938.

HEAL & SON

PHOTO HANS LANGENDORF

design. Another aspect of the criteria for 'modern' design in Modern Movement terms concerned the use of 'new' materials that were the products of industrial technology, particularly metal, glass and laminated wood. These materials could be worked by machine and thus had connotations of mass production; they were therefore seen as appropriate to this century, even though they had been used for furniture long before this[3] (Fig 26). Bentwood chairs, for example, developed by Thonet in the mid-nineteenth century, were much favoured by the exponents of the Modern Movement.

Fig 26: Bentwood furniture, Michael Thonet, from Oetzmann & Co catalogue, London, c1885.

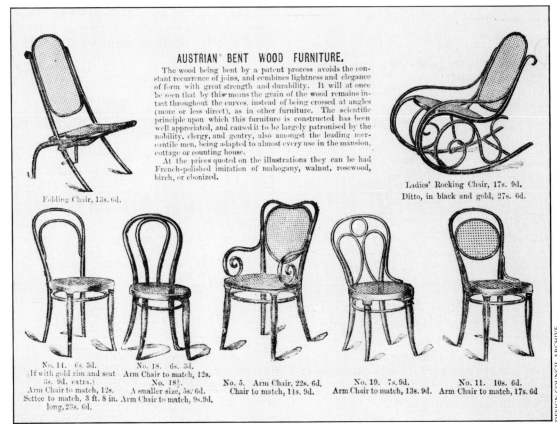

AUSTRIAN BENT WOOD FURNITURE.

The wood being bent by a patent process avoids the constant recurrence of joins, and combines lightness and elegance of form with great strength and durability. It will at once be seen that by this means the grain of the wood remains intact throughout the curves, instead of being crossed at angles (more or less direct), as in other furniture. The scientific principle upon which this furniture is constructed has been well appreciated, and caused it to be largely patronised by the nobility, clergy, and gentry, also amongst the leading mercantile men, being adapted to almost every use in the mansion, cottage or counting house.

At the prices quoted on the illustrations they can be had French-polished imitation of mahogany, walnut, rosewood, birch, or ebonized.

Folding Chair, 13s. 6d.

Ladies' Rocking Chair, 17s. 9d.
Ditto, in black and gold, 27s. 6d.

No. 14. 6s. 3d.
(If with gold rim and seat 3s. 9d. extra.)
Arm Chair to match, 12s.
Settee to match, 3 ft. 8 in. long, 23s. 6d.

No. 18. 6s. 3d.
Arm Chair to match, 12s.
No. 18½.
A smaller size, 5s. 6d.
Arm Chair to match, 9s. 9d.

No. 5. Arm Chair, 22s. 6d.
Chair to match, 11s. 9d.

No. 19. 7s. 9d.
Arm Chair to match, 13s. 9d.

No. 11. 10s. 6d.
Arm Chair to match, 17s. 6d.

The BA Chair and Metal Furniture

The BA chair

The BA chair was light in weight yet it shared none of the characteristics associated with the machine aesthetic. In arriving at this design Race was not concerned with the machine aesthetic or any of the ideas of the avant-garde of the 1930s. The single most important factor influencing the design of the BA chair was the lack of wood. Cast aluminium alloy was used as a substitute for wood at a time when all the traditional furniture materials were in short supply, and it is significant that once these shortages ceased Race did not develop his ideas for cast aluminium furniture further. The first designs for the BA chair used sand-casting for the five components of the chair. A tapering T section was chosen for the leg components so that the greatest strength came at the seat area where it was required. This tapering profile provided savings in weight and cost of materials and also gave the chair a lighter appearance. In addition the main visual surface of the T section could be finished and polished flat fairly easily.

Sand castings have a rough texture and require considerable polishing and finishing if they are to be acceptable in furniture. But because light alloys are comparatively soft and the finishing processes difficult to control, the edges can be removed easily and the precision of the outline can become blurred as a result. To ensure a sharp profile, the first designs for the BA chair imitated the section of a steel T bar (Fig 27).

Two patterns were used for the four leg components as the rear leg was identical to the front but extended upwards in order to receive a curved backrest and was slightly angled (Fig 28). The chair seat frame consisted of a D-shaped rimmed base with two diagonals that provided the fixing positions for the legs. All the bolts were tightened by hand with a torque wrench;[4] electrical equipment for this process

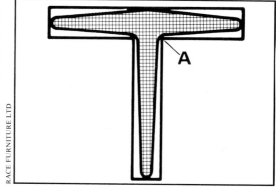

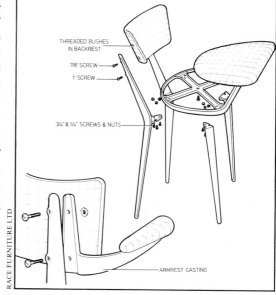

Fig 27, top: The sharp corners of the tapered T section (A) localised stress and resulted in fractures of the flange. These problems were overcome by altering the profile.

Fig 28, above: Components of the BA 3A chair. A plate of thin (14 SWG) aluminium alloy was cut to form the seat. Plywood could not be used because the company had no licence to use wood.

was not introduced into the Clapham factory until about 1960.[5] The cushion material for the seat was rubberised hair. The problem of seat covering was solved by the discovery of quantities of ex-RAF lightweight white cotton duck. This was dyed blue, terracotta or green, cut and sewn to fit the seats and tightened with a drawstring.

The backrest was made from a plate of 14 SWG hardened alloy shaped and blanked with four keyhole slots. Four studs were riveted to the upper parts of the back legs to coincide with

Fig 29: Dining chair BA 2 with back veneered in either mahogany, birch or walnut, 1947.

Specification of the BA 2 chairs from the CoID's 1953 Design Review (now called Design Centre Selection).

the keyhole slots in the backrest plates, and the backrest was then sprung into position. The assembly techniques of the BA chair thus had more in common with those used in car assembly plants than those associated with the furniture industry.[6]

The backrests of the BA chairs relied on the natural spring of the hardened plate to hold them in place, so if one bounced in and out of the chair – even slightly vigorously – the backrest would react and deposit itself on the floor! Customers began complaining and this problem was solved by introducing a small grub screw that locked the backrest into position.[7]

In the first chairs produced the aluminium castings were finished in wax, but after a few months this was replaced by the more efficient and economical process of stove enamelling. A further modification to the production of the BA chair came in 1946 when the sand-casting process was replaced by die-casting. E.C. Lewin, Managing Director of a foundry in Kettering, saw the chair at the 'Britain Can Make It' exhibition organised by the Council of Industrial Design at the Victoria and Albert Museum in 1946 and he suggested that he could pressure die-cast the components. The design of the components was modified to take advantage of the extra strength that resulted from die-casting and this enabled the amount of aluminium alloy used to be reduced by about 25 per cent, halving the factory cost of the chair. In the die-cast version the legs were stronger and more slender, and because die-casting is more accurate than sand casting the finishing was easier.

From the early days the chair was available either with arms (BA 3A) or without (BA 3). By 1947 the supply of wood was more plentiful and the BA 2 was introduced which had a back veneered in a choice of mahogany, birch or walnut (Fig 29).

Aluminium alloy tables and cabinets

To go with the dining chairs, Race designed a range of dining tables (BC 115–118, Fig 30) and a sideboard cabinet (BD 1, Fig 31). These had tops made of Holoplast, a laminated plastic veneered with a highly polished mahogany finish, which was heat and scratch resistant (Fig 32). Indeed, the company catalogue claimed: 'The full beauty of the wood veneers is retained and preserved by a hard, transparent polish which is almost indestructible. It cannot be harmed by dilute acids, boiling water or alcohol drinks and a Race table top is left undamaged even by a burning cigarette end!'[8]

Holoplast had a honeycomb edge that had to be covered in a way that harmonised with both the aluminium legs and the top. The solution was an edging of 'silver-grey aluminium invisibly fastened by a process known only to the makers of Race furniture'.[9] The aluminium loop was heated up and shrunk on to the table or cabinet top, and was then screwed into the edge of the Holoplast with aluminium screws at 3in (7.6cm) intervals. The heads of all the screws were then filed so that they were flush with the aluminium strip, and the aluminium strip and remainder of the screws burnished up so that the individual screws could not be seen.[10]

The problem of fixing the T-section die-cast aluminium legs to the table top was solved by inserting four wooden blocks in the Holoplast for the legs to be screwed into. On the cabinet the legs were not die-cast but hand cut from $\frac{3}{4}$in (1.9cm) aluminium sheet; they were then put in a vice, filed smooth and the edges radiused by hand. A good finish was produced with wire wool and oil and the legs were then bolted into a steel channel.[11] The bodies of the cabinets were of aluminium sheet which was flock-coated on the inside. This involved first coating the inside of the cabinet with glue and then using a 4in (10.16cm) diameter flock gun. When the flock was set, the surplus was brushed off for re-use and the result was rather like baize. The sideboard cabinet was subsequently available in a variety of configurations suitable for office or domestic use (Fig 33).

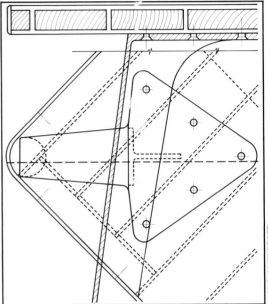

Fig 30, top: Dining table BC 117 and occasional table, 1946. Both had demountable legs of cast aluminium alloy.
Fig 31, above: Sideboard cabinet BD 1, 1946.

Fig 32, top: Section of Holoplast table top.
Fig 33, above: Unit furniture, 1947. The horse on the cabinet formed the basis of the company logo.

'Britain Can Make It'

It was the 'Britain Can Make It' exhibition that was in many ways the making of the company. This exhibition was put on in 1946 by the newly formed Council of Industrial Design (now The Design Council). The aim of the exhibition was to show what British industry could do after the devastating effects of the war, and to stimulate interest and awareness of design among manufacturers and the public. It was one of the first events to be promoted by the Council and it was held in 90,000 square feet (8370 sq m) of the Victoria and Albert Museum, which was empty at the time (Fig 34).

Race had heard of plans for the exhibition and obtained details of it from the Council. The Council was responsible for the choice of every item in the exhibition and Ernest Race Ltd submitted prototype samples. The total number of exhibits shown at the 'Britain Can Make It' exhibition was 5259 and the experience gained by the Council in selecting items for the exhibition was to prove invaluable when it came to the organisation and selection of goods for

DESIGN COUNCIL

Fig 34: Living room from the Britain Can Make It Exhibition, 1946. The upholstered furniture, dark floor and richly patterned curtains gave a feeling of heaviness.

the Festival of Britain five years later. The exhibition was seen by nearly $1\frac{1}{2}$ million visitors and was very successful; the public was interested in good design, though some discontent was expressed when it was found that not all the goods exhibited were available in the shops. Out of the total goods exhibited 36 per cent were available for the home market, $14\frac{1}{2}$ per cent would soon be available, and $23\frac{1}{2}$ per cent would be available later.[12] It is thus perhaps not surprising that the exhibition became known popularly as the 'Britain Can't Have It' exhibition. The 'Britain Can Make It' exhibition showed that the Council of Industrial Design could have an effect on industry and that manufacturers would allow their goods to be selected for exhibition on a competitive basis. The exhibition also gave opportunities to young designers.

The prototypes submitted by Race for the exhibition were examined by a committee that included Anthony Heal and Geoffrey Dunn. Geoffrey Dunn recalled that when he first saw the 'extraordinary aluminium furniture' designed by Ernest Race, he was so taken with it that he went to the Race factory and showrooms. The design of the showrooms was in off-white with coconut matting which provided 'a splendid environment' quite untypical of those days. As a result of that visit the company received its first order for furniture to be sold by Geoffrey Dunn's shop in Bromley. This was followed very shortly by one from Heal and Son. Geoffrey Dunn had in fact met Ernest Race before the war, when he had sold some of his designs for Indian fabrics in his shop, and they shared a common interest in vintage motor cars.[13]

One of the first large orders the company received was for 1500 chairs and tables for troop-ships that were bringing home demobilised servicemen. The strength and

lightness of the furniture was stressed in advertisements (Fig 35), and its resistance to all extremes of climate and most insects. In the civilian area the furniture was chosen by Misha Black for the Ceylon Tea Centre in Regent Street, London, and it was used in many restaurants throughout the country (Figs 36, 37 and 38). In 1954 Race was awarded the Gold Medal for the BA 3 chair at the Tenth Triennale in Milan. Further awards made to British designers that year included a Gold Medal to

Fig 35: Advertisement for the BA chairs in Shipbuilding and Shipping Record, *May 1957. The special ferrules to make the chairs silent were a later addition.*

Fig 36, left: Tea lounge at the Ceylon Tea Centre, London, Design Research Unit, 1958. Two types of table were used, the BC 117 and a three-legged triangular version.
Fig 37, bottom: Cafeteria at Littlewoods Store, Liverpool, 1956. Note the ferrules on the chairs.
Fig 38, below: Lyons self-service teashop, Lower Regent Street, London, Richard Lionel-Hands Associates, 1951.

DRU/JOHN MALTBY

J. LYONS & CO

LITTLEWOODS

Robin Day for the design of Hille furniture, the Gran Premio – the highest award – to Lucienne Day for textile design, a Gold Medal to Lucie Rie and Hans Coper for their ceramics, and a Silver Medal to John Reid for light fittings. In addition Race was awarded a Silver Medal for his Antelope chair (see page 44).

Several companies were involved in designing and producing aluminium furniture in this early post-war period 1945–7, when there were little or no supplies of wood for traditional furniture making (Figs 39, 40 and 41).

DESIGN COUNCIL

ESA LTD

PARKER-KNOLL LTD/HAROLD WHITE

Fig 39, top left: Plymet aluminium alloy furniture, Clive Latimer, 1946 (Heal & Son).
Fig 40, left: Aluminium alloy 'Toledo' chair, c1949 (Parker-Knoll).
Fig 41, above: Junior table desk and chairs in laminated plywood and aluminium alloy, J. W. Leonard, 1948 (Esavian).

The Festival Chairs and Contemporary Design

The 'Britain Can Make It' exhibition in 1946 set the company of Ernest Race Ltd on the path to success, if not to fortune, but it was the Festival of Britain in 1951 that brought the work of Race to the attention of a much greater number of people. Of all the furniture designed by him, probably the most familiar items are the chairs he designed for the Festival, the Antelope and the Springbok. Indeed, even today when people who visited the South Bank site are shown photographs they mostly reply: 'Oh yes, I remember those, they were such fun!' (Figs 42, 43, 44 and 45).

The Festival was many things. If it introduced 'modern' design to the public for the first time then there were distinct differences between the 'modern' of the Modern Movement and that of the design at the Festival. It coined many new terms that came to have specific stylistic connotations. Chief among these terms were 'contemporary' and 'Festival of Britain', as in 'It's very Festival of Britain', which could refer to a building, a piece of furniture, an interior or a product. For a while in the early 1950s these terms 'Festival of Britain' and 'contemporary' were virtually interchangeable.

'Contemporary' design in today's understanding of the term implies a preference for organic forms that betray a somewhat immoral voluptuousness (Figs 46, 47 and 48).

Today it also implies the juxtaposition of forms that do not relate to each other, as in these chairs (Figs 49 and 50) and in Ralph Tubbs's Dome of Discovery (Fig 51). All feature a massive body and slender means of support, and the contrast between them is very evident. However, in the mid-1950s this would have been termed 'contemporistic' design rather than 'contemporary'.

'Contemporistic' implied the use of certain physical features associated with 'contemporary' design, such as metal legs, but the whole object did not appear to be an integrated design and there was a discontinuity between the form of the body and the means of support. In the 1950s not only was 'contemporistic' design distinguished from 'contemporary' design, there was also reproduction 'contemporary'. This used traditional forms but in such a way that lightness was emphasised (Fig 52). The length of the legs and the way in which they splayed gave the effect of floating to the body of the chair or cabinet that they were supporting.

In the 1950s the connotations of 'contemporary' were not restricted to characteristics of style, they referred to the whole basis of design. 'Contemporary' design was 'well engineered, soundly constructed, efficient and – thanks to mass production – cheap!'[1] The aims of 'contemporary' design thus had much in common with those of the Modern Movement: simplicity, honest expression of materials, no ornament. 'Contemporary' design was what many people bought and put in their homes, it was available to a wide income range, and it was treated seriously. It is worth exploring how this change in meaning has occurred.

The period of 'contemporary' design, the late 1940s and 1950s, was one of economic expansion in Britain. By 1964 there had been nearly a quarter century of full employment, with unemployment averaging less than two per cent. (In the 1930s unemployment averaged 16 per cent and in the 1920s 11 per cent.) Between 1950 and 1964 Britain's Gross Domestic Product (GDP) grew at an average of three per cent. This was an improvement over its growth between the wars of less than two per cent, though it was not as good as the growth in GDP in Germany, France, Italy and Japan in the period 1950–64 of five per cent or more.[2] It is this expanding economy that provided the

DESIGN COUNCIL

MANOR STUDIO

DESIGN COUNCIL

Race furniture at the Festival of Britain.

Fig 42, opposite, above: Springbok chairs at the Fairway cafe near the main entrance from Waterloo.

Fig 43, opposite, below: Antelope chairs on the terrace of the Regatta Restaurant, with a view of the Bailey Bridge.

Fig 44, left: Antelope chairs outside the Lion and Unicorn Pavilion.

Fig 45, below: Antelope chairs and tables in the cafe of the Homes and Gardens Pavilion.

DESIGN COUNCIL

RACE FURNITURE LTD

H. K. FURNITURE LTD

Fig 46, above: Easy chair DA 1, Ernest Race, 1949 (designed 1946).
Fig 47, above right: 'Sabu' wing chair, Howard Keith, 1947.
Fig 48, right: Homemaker plate, c1952. Note the organic forms of the boomerang table and the double seat.

DESIGN COUNCIL

Fig 49, left: Chair by Ico Parisi, from the Tenth Triennale, Milan, 1954.
Fig 50, below left: Chair, A. & R. Duckworth, 1956.
Fig 51, below: Dome of Discovery, Festival of Britain, Ralph Tubbs, 1951.
Note the contrast between the apparently massive bodies of all three, and the slender supports.

DESIGN COUNCIL

DESIGN COUNCIL

DESIGN COUNCIL ARCHIVE

context for the search for new materials and new forms for a widening domestic market that was so important to the development of 'contemporary' design.

Many of the ideas that were greeted as new in the 1950s had been current among avant-garde designers in the 1930s, but the hiatus of the Second World War meant that they were not widely developed until they were rediscovered by the new generation of designers in the post-war period. The sources of 'contemporary' design must thus be sought in the pre-war period. Eileen Gray's free-form table (Fig 53), with its contrast between the massive top and the slender means of support, shows many of the qualities that came to be associated with 'contemporistic' design in the mid-1950s, while the organic forms of 'contemporary' design can be seen in McKnight Kauffer's poster for the exhibition held by the MARS Group at Burlington Galleries in 1937 (Fig 54).

The sources for 'contemporary' and 'contemporistic' design could also be seen in the fine arts of the period: in the surrealistic paintings of Joán Miro or Ben Nicholson, with their emphasis on disconnected elements (Fig 55); and in Barbara Hepworth's and Henry Moore's organic sculptures (Fig 56).

The sources for 'contemporary' design thus lie in the pre-war period and, in contrast with the Modern Movement 'contemporary' design, favoured organic as well as rectilinear and geometric forms and these forms could be seen in furniture and in textiles (Figs 57 and 58).

ODHAMS PRESS LTD

Fig 52: Reproduction 'contemporary' shown in Modern Homes Illustrated *by F. R. Yerbury, 1947. The long splayed legs gave a floating feeling to the furniture.*

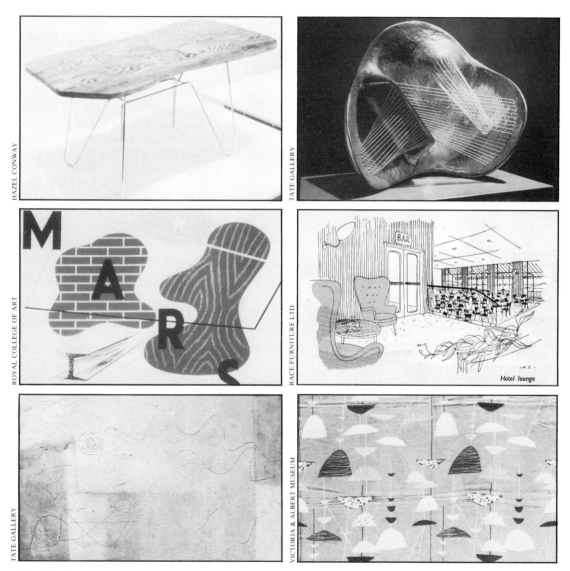

HAZEL CONWAY

TATE GALLERY

ROYAL COLLEGE OF ART

RACE FURNITURE LTD

Hotel lounge

TATE GALLERY

VICTORIA & ALBERT MUSEUM

Fig 53, top: Free-form table, Eileen Gray, 1938.
Fig 54, centre: Poster for MARS exhibition, 1937.
Fig 55, above: 'Painting', Ben Nicholson, 1932.

Fig 56, top: 'Stringed Figure', Henry Moore, 1938.
Fig 57, centre: Ernest Race Ltd catalogue, 1947.
Fig 58, above: 'Calyx' linen, Lucienne Day, 1951.

Another of the developments that influenced 'contemporary' furniture was the application of materials such as plastics and laminated wood, which could be moulded into shapes impossible to achieve with solid wood. The work of Aalto, Breuer and others in the development and use of plywood and laminated wood furniture was well known among architects and designers in the 1930s (see Figs 7 and 8). Concern for the development of these materials was illustrated by the 'Organic Design in Home Furnishings' competition held by the Museum of Modern Art in New York in 1940, in which first prizes were won by Eames and Saarinen (Fig 59).

It was not, however, until after the war that furniture using such materials was introduced more widely to the public in Britain. When this furniture was introduced, it was thought by many to be flimsy (Fig 60). Plywood and laminated wood are very strong and can be used to produce light elegant pieces that in solid wood would be structurally unsound. Thus the criticism of flimsiness was largely unfounded, due primarily to a lack of understanding of the properties of the material. The introduction of

MOMA, NEW YORK

DESIGN COUNCIL

FRITZ HANSENS EFTEL

Fig 59, above left: Organic Design Exhibition, Museum of Modern Art, New York, 1941. Furniture by Charles Eames and Eero Saarinen.
Fig 60, left: Laminated beech table and chairs, Arne Jacobsen, c1953. Note the thin section of the chairs.
Fig 61, above: Living room from Unity House, Ideal Home Exhibition, 1950. All the furniture was raised from the ground, giving an effect of lightness compared with Figure 34.

solid metal rod legs to furniture was another example of the same thinking. In the 1950s most people thought of furniture in terms of traditional materials, with the proportions and appearance that resulted from the use of solid wood. When faced with a solid metal leg their first reaction – the result of a subconscious comparison with wood – was that it was too thin to support the table or chair.

In the organic forms of 1950s 'contemporary' design we can see the designer reacting to some of the forms that have evolved out of the use of 'new' materials such as plastics and plywood, and there is a conscious attempt to achieve the lightness possible with them (Fig 61). This does not mean that he was deliberately copying ideas from other materials, but rather that he was absorbing and reacting to new design ideas. To the majority of people it was the Festival of

Fig 62: General view of the Festival of Britain, 1951, showing the Skylon (Powell & Moya) and the Dome of Discovery (Ralph Tubbs).

Britain that first introduced them to 'contemporary' design.

The initial idea was to hold an international exhibition to commemorate the Great Exhibition of 1851. However, this proved to be more an excuse to hold a festival rather than the reason. The real motive behind holding the Festival was to boost morale after the war and continuing shortages, and to symbolise faith in the future. The idea for an international fair was dropped and instead plans were put forward for a British trade exhibition and an exhibition of the arts. In London the Festival was to be sited on the South Bank of the River Thames (the area now occupied by the Shell Centre, Hayward Gallery and National Theatre); there were to be pleasure gardens at Battersea and local events throughout the country so that the whole of the UK was involved. The theme of the South Bank exhibition was 'The Land and the People' and it was designed to show the ingenuity of the British in using the resources available to them.

'. . . This is a narrative exhibition . . . (which) tells the story of British contributions to world civilisations in the arts of peace.'[3] To sustain the narrative idea, each pavilion was laid out in a particular order and each was so designed as to give a foretaste of the story that it told: 'The Land of Britain', 'The People of Britain', and 'The Dome of Discovery'. The appearance of each building was related to its contents and, although this approach might have led to a lack of overall harmony, integration was achieved by means of grouping, contrasts of colours, textures and silhouette, and above all 'by the background of trees, gardens, fountains and flowers against which all the buildings are set';[4] a picturesque approach (Fig 62).

In Sir Gordon Russell's view the Peter Shepheard gardens were some of the best things at the Festival and 'the presence of similar chairs all over the site gave the whole a coherence', reinforcing the integrating role of the landscape.[5] These included Race's Antelope and Springbok chairs, which were used both indoors and out for restaurant and public seating. Race recalled being told by Sir Hugh Casson, the coordinating architect for the whole Festival, that during the preparations the word 'style' was not used once because it was assumed that everyone would be working in an up-to-date style.[6] Architects and designers were working in the same direction, which Race thought was inevitable as 'the architectural theme of the day sets the pattern for thinking throughout the rest of design. After all, other equipment has to be designed to fit inside contemporary architecture.'[7]

The way in which goods were chosen for display at the Festival was quite different from that of any previous exhibition, except for 'Britain Can Make It'. All other previous large-scale national and international exhibitions had been organised in trade sections and space was sold to firms to display what they wished, as they wished. At the Festival there was no space to let and no goods were displayed unless they reached a standard of design satisfactory to the Council of Industrial Design.

The role of the Council of Industrial Design (CoID) under the Directorship of Sir Gordon Russell cannot be overestimated, for it was the source of all manufactured objects. Not only did the Council select all exhibits, but it also worked out the detailed themes to be presented in the various South Bank pavilions.

The first stage in the CoID's selection of exhibits was a survey of products, undertaken in cooperation with trade and research associations, industrialists and manufacturers. The next stage was an illustrated index of the best current designs. In January 1949 all manufacturers were invited to submit photographs of what they considered to be their best current designs. The CoID did not select the products that sold best, but those which, in their opinion, reached the highest standards of 'contemporary' design, and their assessment covered functional, aesthetic and engineering qualities. These criteria were very much those of the 'fitness for purpose' ideal promoted by the Design and Industries Association before the war – the CoID certainly did not see itself promoting the machine aesthetic or Bauhaus design. From this information the 1951 Stock List was compiled which provided the Festival designers with a reference for ideas and exhibits.

The CoID controlled not only the selection of exhibits but also the design of all public facilities in the Festival, including the public seating. Designs for this furniture were submitted to the Council and 'the designs of Ernest Race were well ahead of all others submitted'.[8]

Springbok

The aim in this design was to produce a chair that could be left outside if necessary, but which was also comfortable and soft to sit on. The intention was that it could also be used indoors, so breaking down the hitherto rigid distinction between indoor and outdoor furniture. The Springbok's frame was of $\frac{1}{2}$in (1.27cm) mild steel rod, stove enamelled white (Fig 63). The front and back legs formed one piece, the seat and back frame also formed one piece. The ball feet were of cast aluminium stove enamelled white to match the frame. The seat and back were of springs covered in heavy gauge PVC tubing, available in red, yellow, blue or grey.

These springs were fastened to the frame by steel strips, also clad in PVC tube, which were kept equidistant by a continuous wire distance-piece on each side (Fig 64). The springs needed to be fairly readily replaceable as they tended to

Fig 63, left: Springbok chairs at the South
Bank Exhibition, Festival of Britain, 1951.
Fig 64, below left: Detail of Springbok
construction.
Fig 65, below: Stacked Springboks, yellow chair
on top, red and blue underneath. All the feet
were white regardless of the colour of the seat.

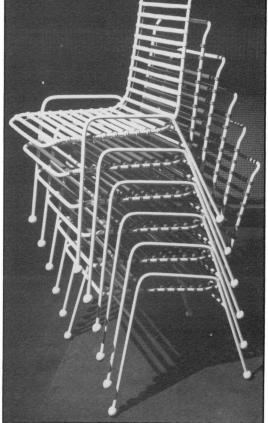

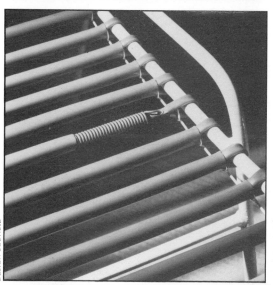

sag after heavy use, but this design made replacement difficult. However, this was not seen as a problem for the Festival, but more for the long-term use of the chairs.

In order to make the chairs stackable, the front and back leg component on each side came outside the frame; this caused great pressure between the back upright rod and the seat rod, and as a result the weld tended to fail here. This fault could have been put right, but the design and production of the chairs for the Festival took place within a very short time. Indeed, the company did not take on additional staff for the Festival and the normal staff of about 17 people in the factory and five in the office worked very long hours to produce the Festival orders[9] (Fig 65). Evidence of Sir Gordon Russell's confidence in Race's design, in spite of these criticisms, can be seen in the fact that he still had Springbok chairs on the terrace of his garden, though by 1979 the yellow plastic had faded to a pale cream!

Antelope

This chair was available in a single and a double version (Fig 66) and like the Springbok was designed specially for the Festival. Its frame was of welded mild steel rods of $\frac{1}{4}$in, $\frac{3}{8}$in and $\frac{1}{2}$in (0.63cm, 0.93cm, 1.27cm) rustproofed and stove-enamelled white (Fig 67). The seat was of plywood with holes drilled in strategic positions to prevent rainwater settling on it. These seats were brought in from Aylesbury Bros and were available in yellow, blue, red and grey. Like the Springbok the Antelope had white ball feet.

These ball feet served a practical function, for without anything at their ends the thin metal legs would have damaged the surfaces they stood on and could have hurt people's feet. The legs with their ball feet had much in common visually with atomic structures and models for atoms and electrons (Figs 68 and 69).

In 1949 the Society of Industrial Artists (SIA) held a weekend course to introduce designers to visual material from the arts and sciences, and it

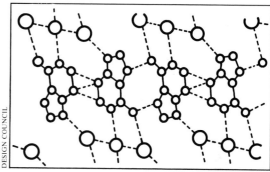

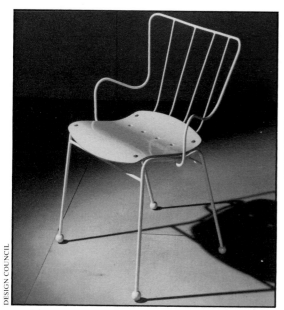

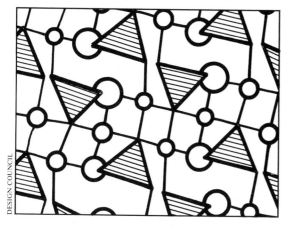

Fig 66, opposite: Single and double Antelopes at the Vale of Leven Hospital, Dumbartonshire, 1955.
Fig 67, top: Single Antelope, 1950.
Fig 68, above: Atomic model of afwillite.
Fig 69, top right: Atomic model of adenine hydrochloride.

was here that Dr Kathleen Lonsdale had read a paper on crystallography and suggested that these might form the basis for designs. The work of the Festival Pattern Group proposed by Mark Hartland Thomas of the CoID did indeed lead to the design of wallpapers, pottery and textiles based on atomic structures (Fig 70), and it is highly likely that Race – a fellow of the SIA since 1947 – was aware of these events (Fig 71).

The Antelope was less comfortable than the Springbok to sit on, which may have been due to a deliberate request by the organisers to prevent people lingering too long on them.[10] Despite this, it was this chair that caught the imagination of the public: its gaiety, elegance and wit seemed to encapsulate their feelings about the Festival. Moreover it caught the imagination of architects and its popularity can be judged by its appearance both indoors and out in architectural journals of the 1950s.

The lightness and strength of the Antelope, which could only have been achieved with the particular materials used, seemed to typify what 'contemporary' design should aim for. From the stylistic point of view the slightly splayed steel rod legs came to be one of the characteristics associated with 'contemporary' design as the 1950s progressed (Fig 72).

Because of the popularity of the Antelope chair, the influences on Race's design have been the subject of some debate. Criticisms were levelled at the Antelope for being frivolous and for not being 'modern' in the sense of the Modern Movement. Were its spindly form and splay legs derived from Charles Eames's steel and plywood chair LCM–1 (see Fig 100)? This chair was well known in England from magazines, and examples of it had appeared by 1950,[11] but it seems unlikely to have been the

Fig 70, top: Screen-printed cotton, Warner & Sons, 1951. The design was derived from the crystal structure of haemoglobin.
Fig 71, above: Screen at South Bank Exhibition.
Fig 72, above right: 'The Orrery' coffee bar, London, Terence Conran, c1955.
Fig 73, right: Easy chair DA 2, 1949.

main influence. An examination of Race's earlier work using welded steel rod for furniture indicated the source for his ideas. The link between the Antelope and the Race easy chair (DA 2, Fig 73) becomes apparent if the

upholstery is stripped away (Fig 74). Both are made of welded steel rod and the forms of the rods are very similar. The Antelope is indeed the skeleton of an easy chair. The production of Antelope chairs with ball feet continued until 1957, when the ball feet were replaced by moulded plastic ferrules (Fig 75).[12]

The Antelope table had a plywood top and legs of drawn steel tube, with ball feet.[13] It was one of the few examples of Race's use of this material; another was his bar stool, BS 3 (1956), which had legs of stove-enamelled tapered steel tube. Race had previously designed a bar stool, BS 2, in 1951, but this had legs of tapered T-section die-cast aluminium alloy and stiffening struts of the same material.[14] Another design that used steel tube and steel rod was a chair for spastic children (Fig 76). The solid rubber wheels allowed the chair to be manoeuvred, and the swivel wheel in front prevented it from tipping forward too far.[15]

Fig 74, top: Sectional view of easy chair.
Fig 75, above: Plastic ferrule, 1958.
Fig 76, right: Chair for spastic child, 1953.

Steel Rod Furniture

It is in the area of the application of steel rod to furniture design that Race's contribution as a furniture designer was significant. 'Race in steel and Aalto in wood represent a reasonable approach to quantity production.'[1]

The development of welded steel rod furniture by Race stems from 1946, for while the company was manufacturing cast aluminium furniture it was looking for new areas of development both in terms of material and in terms of new ranges of furniture. One reason for the development of welded steel furniture was that steel rod was available, furthermore the company liked to keep as much control over production as possible. The diecasting for the cast aluminium furniture had to be done outside, whereas welded steel rod furniture could be produced completely on the company premises.

Upholstered chairs

What areas of furniture should the new developments cover? Noel Jordan recalled: 'On one occasion we spent practically a whole day with Mr Christopher Heal who suggested the next main development in our range, and that was for easy chairs and settees.'[2] The range produced – all of which qualified as Utility – included an easy chair (DA 2, see Fig 73) with a 5ft (1.5m) long settee to match (DA 4, Fig 77), a wing chair DA 1, Fig 78) with a high-back settee to match (DA 5, Fig 79), and an executive office desk chair (DA 3).[3] Each consisted of a welded steel frame that was light in weight and rigid, a coil sprung seat and upholstery of hair and latex foam. The first versions of these chairs had die-cast aluminium legs, stove-enamelled in cream/grey; these were subsequently replaced by ʌurned wooden legs.

Compared with some of the bulky pre-war upholstered furniture (Fig 80), when these designs appeared they seemed light in weight and volume, and thus 'modern' and 'contemporary' (Fig 81). The use of steel rods and the method of upholstery enabled more delicate pieces to be produced, with just the attributes that were associated with 'contemporary' design in the 1950s: '. . . welded metal rods (allow) a construction admirable for the more delicately shaped contemporary chair'.[4] In Figure 82 this lightness is further emphasised by the standard lamp and table lamp of steel rod and the plain carpet and walls.

Subsequently a ladies' chair was added to this range to meet the need for an easy chair without arms for use when sewing and knitting (Fig 83). Wood was still expensive at this time and Noel Jordan got hold of some packing crates which were broken up and used; kipper boxes, boxes stamped Tate and Lyle, nothing was wasted, everything was painted with dark green paint before being upholstered.[5]

The Woodpecker (Fig 84) – developed from the ladies' chair the following year – was of substantially the same dimensions to suit smaller people, but its legs were fitted inside the frame of the seat, whereas the legs of the ladies' chair were fixed to the outside of the frame. This construction feature gave the Woodpecker flat sides, so several chairs could be arranged alongside each other to form a settee. A small amendment to the basic design thus introduced a wider range of flexibility, with minimum expenditure on production costs.

For the production of the cast aluminium furniture working drawings were essential because the casting was done outside the company (though the drawings were produced after the basic design had been arrived at). For the metal rod furniture Race did not evolve his designs through a series of drawings, but rather more empirically, in conjunction with the workshop manager Johnny Hansford. Race would produce a design in, say, drinking straws

DESIGN COUNCIL ARCHIVE

RACE FURNITURE LTD

DESIGN COUNCIL

*Fig 77, above left: Settee DA 4 with welded
steel frame and coil sprung seat, 1946.*
*Fig 78, centre left: Wing chair DA 1 with cast
aluminium legs and coffee table BB 15, 1946.*
*Fig 79, below left: High-back settee DA 5, 1949
version with turned wooden legs. The original
1946 version had cast aluminium legs.*
Fig 80, below: 'Modernistic' from Here of
All Places *by Osbert Lancaster, 1969.*

JOHN MURRAY PUBLISHERS LTD

DESIGN COUNCIL

from which Johnny would produce a prototype. Race would then make adjustments to the prototype – but never more than one at a time – until he was satisfied with it. The finalised prototype would then become the model for production and from it Johnny would work out the specification, dimensions, materials required, size of rods to be used and lengths, form of jigs etc.[6] All the steel rod furniture was produced by cold bending the steel rod on a jig (Figs 85, 86 and 87). Although at first sight it might appear that each chair and settee required a separate jig, this was not in fact the case. For example, the forms of the DA 4 settee were those of two halves of the DA 2 chair (see Figs 73 and 77) with a bar welded in between, and the two-seater Antelope was produced in a similar way from the single-seat Antelope.

Fig 81, above: Living room, 1952, showing the contrast between the bulky pre-1939 furniture and the more delicate 'contemporary' furniture. Clockwise, from left: DA 1 wing chair, wooden dining chair, radiogram, traditional armchair, coffee table (Ward & Austin), DA 4 settee, two-tiered table (Finmar), wooden-armed chair (prototype, Utility Furniture Panel).

Fig 82, opposite, top: Living/dining room at the Ideal Home Exhibition, 1949, furnished by the CoID with DA 1 wing chair and DA 4 settee.

Fig 83, opposite, below left: Ladies' chair, 1951, available in both low and high-backed versions and stackable.

Fig 84, opposite, below right: Woodpecker chair, 1952. These could be placed together to form a settee.

DESIGN COUNCIL

RACE FURNITURE LTD

RACE FURNITURE LTD

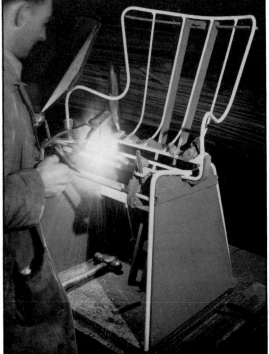

Figs 85 and 86, left: Cold bending steel rod for the Antelope chair.
Fig 87, above: Welding the frame of the Antelope chair.

Steel rod rocking chair

The gauge of solid steel rod necessary to make sufficiently strong furniture is much smaller than that required if tubular metal is used, and solid section metal – whether of steel or aluminium alloys – can be bent in far smaller radii than tube, thus allowing a greater variety of forms and increasing the potential design flexibility (Fig 88). As Race became more familiar with the potential for welded steel rod furniture, so he developed designs that exploited this. The steel rod rocking chair was designed in 1948 (Fig 89). The lightness and strength of this design could only have been achieved with the particular material used. In Race's view, if a design for a particular material could be copied in another material, then the designer had failed to exploit the potential of the original material thoroughly.[7] Although welding was a well established technique, very few designers were designing furniture that could only be welded. Race understood welding and designed very much with this in mind; welding depends greatly on workmanship and he saw possibilities that could not have been achieved by any other methods. In particular, welding gave the opportunity for lightness, which is very important for portable furniture such as chairs.

The Antelope and Springbok chairs (1950), the Heron easy chair (1955) and the Flamingo (1957), which won a Design Centre Award in 1959, were all based on welded steel rod and illustrated the flexibility of form possible.

Heron and Flamingo

The Heron (Fig 90) was based on a welded steel frame, Pirelli webbing and latex foam cushioning for both the chair and the loose cushions. The link between the design of the Heron and that of the Dormouse settee (Fig 91) is evident, particularly in the shape of the arms. The Dormouse however used vertical coil springing in the seat, not Pirelli webbing. It is yet another example of how Race approached design, refining and developing an idea as fully as possible. In the DA range, the Dormouse, the Heron and the Flamingo, Race was seeking to exploit the potential of the steel rod frame for upholstered furniture.

The Flamingo (Fig 92) varied from the Heron in the form and fixing of the wooden legs, and it did not have removable cushions. The materials of its construction were identical to those of the Heron, but as it did not have a removable seat cushion the outline of the seat had greater visual clarity. A settee was also available (Fig 93).

In 1959 the Flamingo chair was chosen for a Design Centre Award, because its 'skilful use of up-to-date materials [steel frame and foam sheeting] help to give it an interesting form', and also because the chair had the 'unusual advantage of being comfortable however you sit in it – straight backed or sprawling'.[8] Despite this award Race is reputed to have preferred the design of the earlier Heron.[9]

The Flamingo and the Heron ranges continued in production until 1961. In 1962 the factory moved to Sheerness on the Isle of Sheppey and a new range of furniture was developed to replace them. One of the reasons for this change was that skilled upholsterers were required to make these ranges. When the factory moved, these skilled men did not move with the company and production had to be altered to use the skills that were available.

The Flamingo, Heron and the earlier DA range of easy chairs illustrated the influence of new materials on 'contemporary' design. Latex foam on a steel rod frame enabled the designer to design forms of comfortable seating that would have been impossible within the limitations imposed by traditional springing and stuffing, for latex foam could be moulded into almost any shape. As a result the designer could

Fig 88, left: 'De Plano' stacking chair with GRP seat, John D. Vale, 1953 (F. Lewis & Sons).
Fig 89, below left: Rocking chair, 1948. White enamelled frame, mahogany arm-rests, removable padded seat on a wooden frame and removable back cushion. A $\frac{3}{4}$in (1.9cm) steel strip welded to the rockers prevented floor damage.
Fig 90, below: Heron chair, 1955. The legs were turned from square-section steel and were available in a range of finishes. They were fitted with Armstrong glides and were removable for packing. Generous proportions—2ft 9in high, 3ft 2in deep, 2ft 7$\frac{1}{2}$in wide (83.8cm × 96.5cm × 80cm)—gave versatility in sitting positions. A footstool was also available.

DESIGN COUNCIL

DESIGN COUNCIL

RACE FURNITURE LTD

design chairs whose forms could be sculptured to fit the body's needs, and which were much lighter than those possible with conventional upholstery. These forms illustrate the search to exploit the potential of new materials within a vocabulary that we can identify as 'contemporary'. The designers' response to the challenge of new materials such as plastics and laminated wood can also be seen in the designs of Eames, Saarinen, Aalto and others of the 1930s and 1940s (Figs 94, 95 and 96). The link between these forms and those of 'contemporary' design is apparent.

Some of Race's developments in welded steel rod furniture were more successful than others. An ingenious though short-lived design was the rocking chair of welded steel rod, the Kangaroo (Fig 97). These chairs, together with nesting coffee tables, were supplied for use on the terrace of the prestigious London offices of Time Life, which was the first large post-war office building to be erected in England (Architect: Michael Rosenauer).[10] The seat and back of the Kangaroo were made from one continuous piece of rod which was bent on a jig. Production presented certain problems due to the length of rod involved in each chair, and only by keeping the factory door open could these lengths be accommodated! The three-strut

DESIGN COUNCIL

DESIGN COUNCIL

DESIGN COUNCIL

Fig 91, above left: Dormouse settee, 1953.
Fig 92, left: Flamingo chair, 1957. Dimensions: 3ft 1in high, 2ft 9in deep, 2ft 9in wide (94cm × 83.8cm × 93.8cm). The Heron seat was deeper as it had a loose cushion.
Fig 93, above: Flamingo settee, 1957.

support reduced the weight of the chair and there was less rigidity when sitting on it than could have been achieved with four struts. However, the main problem of this design was the stress that the single strut at the front of the chair was subject to. As a result it was liable to snap.[11]

Another short-lived exercise in steel rod was the Unicorn three-legged stacking chair plus Gazelle table[12] designed for the British pavilion at the 1958 Brussels World's Fair. This chair was found to be unstable and was withdrawn from production shortly after the exhibition (Fig 98).

HEAL & SON

ERHARD RASMUSSEN

HERMAN MILLER

Fig 94, left: GRP armchair with wire legs, Charles Eames, 1949 (Herman Miller). The contrast between the slender legs and the apparently massive body had much in common with the 'contemporistic' designs of Figures 49 and 50.
Fig 95, top: Armchair and occasional table, Peter Hvidt and O. Mølgaarde Nielsen, c1950.
Fig 96, above: Chair and table, cherry wood frame with redwood top, Borge Mogensen, c1948. The organic forms of Figures 95 and 96 have much in common with those of Figures 46, 47 and 48.

Fig 97, left: Kangaroo rocking chair, 1953.
Fig 98, below: Unicorn chairs and Gazelle table, 1957.

Roebuck

A far more successful design was the Roebuck stacking chair (Fig 99), designed as a low-cost, durable nesting chair, for use indoors or out. Its success can be measured by the fact that it was still in production in 1968, with only minor adjustments to its dimensions and different fittings to the ends of the legs (the balls on the ends of the legs were replaced by moulded plastic ferrules).

The Roebuck had much in common with Eames's LCM-1 chair (Fig 100), for both used the same materials – steel rod and plywood. However, there are significant differences between the two designs. The emphasis in the LCM-1 chair, by virtue of the dimensions of the seat, back and legs, is a horizontal one, that of the Roebuck is vertical. The legs of the Roebuck are longer, the distance between the back panel and the seat is greater and this is emphasised by the two struts supporting the back panel. The LCM-1's back panel has only one strut and the back almost appears to be floating by comparison. There is very little visual emphasis on the frame of the LCM-1 as, apart from the legs and the back strut, it is invisible; it is the seat and back panel that command attention. In the Roebuck attention is drawn to the back, the seat and the frame. The frame is quite visible and the seat can be seen to be resting on it at the front and at the sides. The frame is further emphasised by the balls on the ends of the legs, which draw the eye to them. The seat of the LCM-1 is attached to the frame by one

Fig 99: Roebuck stacking chair, 1951. Plywood seat and back finished in red, yellow, blue or grey enamel, steel rod frame finished in grey or white.

Fig 100: LCM–1 chair, Charles Eames, 1946. Plywood seat, frame of polished chrome.

horizontal bar linking the two front legs, and the back of the seat floats, thus providing springiness when sitting. Similarly, the one strut at the back and rubber mounts provide a degree of springiness when leaning back. The Roebuck is far more rigid, there is no springiness in the seat and only a very slight degree of springiness in the back.

It is impossible to tell whether Race was directly influenced by Eames's design, but the visual similarities between the two chairs have led some commentators to conclude that he was. However, the use of similar materials, such as metal rod and plywood, is likely to produce solutions that superficially appear to have much in common. A closer analysis, as above, shows that in fact the differences are significant.

The range and complexity of shapes possible with steel rod was enormous (Figs 101, 102 and 103), and this was one reason why Race, unlike many of his contemporaries, never experimented with glass fibre. A further, even more significant factor was the cost involved in tooling up for glass fibre production. These would have been very high for such a small company and such a large investment would have necessitated longer production runs and more factory space than that available at Clapham.

Fig 101, top right: Perforated steel and steel rod chair from the Festival of Britain, A. J. Milne, 1951 (Heal & Son).
Fig 102, centre right: 'Grasshopper' flattened, expanded steel and steel rod bench, Nigel Walters, 1953 (A. A. Pegram).
Fig 103, right: 'Rockon' garden rocking chair, steel rod, canvas seat, wooden rockers, Terence Conran, 1953 (Conran Furniture).

Contract Furniture

The production of domestic furniture for sale through shops occupies a large part of the furniture industry, but not the whole of it. Contract furniture for government departments, offices, schools, universities, hospitals, hotels and shipping lines covers a very wide field, much of it is of a very specialised nature, and it generally needs to be more robust than its domestic counterpart as it is often subject to very heavy use. The design of contract furniture is often closely allied to interior design, for in, say, an hotel, shop or ship the furnishing and interior decor go hand in hand. Moreover, buyers from the professional and commercial concerns who commission contract furniture are often more prepared to accept advanced design ideas, and thus it can offer more scope to the designer than is possible in the more conservative domestic area of furniture.

Neptune
Race's Neptune deck-chair (Figs 104 and 105) marked the entry of the company into the field of contract furniture. This chair was one of several commissioned from Ernest Race Ltd by P & O for the Orient Line. To pinpoint a particular work of a designer as being his most original design is liable to raise more questions than it answers. Nevertheless, in terms of form, material and economy of solution to a particular problem, the Neptune stacking and folding chair could perhaps be considered as qualifying as one of Race's most original designs. The design requested for the Neptune was for a modern counterpart of the Victorian deck-chair, to be used on exposed areas of ships and folded and stacked away when not in use. Deck-chairs receive little maintenance, and the Orient Line had found from experience that if brass was used for the hinges, the pins usually seized up; this was the only technical information provided.

An ocean liner travels in a few days from its cold, damp winter port to the heat of the tropical sun. The deck chairs had not only to be able to withstand these extreme climatic changes, but also the salt water and caustic soda solutions used to wash down the decks. The material Race used for his first designs for the Neptune was a plywood of beech laminate bonded with a urea-formaldehyde waterproof adhesive.

Race had experimented as early as 1951[1] with the possibilities of using plywood for an easy chair. The prototype Sprawler chair (Fig 106) had a back and arms of laminated wood 'petals' radiating up and out from the seat, a foam rubber cushion and cast aluminium legs. It was called Sprawler because there was no fixed direction for sitting in it, but it never went into production, possibly because the cost would have been too high.

The thinking behind the forms used for the Neptune was that the same profile could be used for both the seat and the back with consequent saving on the costs of moulds. Ergonomics would imply that such an idea is impracticable, but mock-ups confirmed that Race's idea was sound (Fig 107). It is this concern to re-think a design problem right through – refusing to accept what appear to be obvious limitations – in order to arrive at the best possible solution, that is the mark of a really good designer.

For the seat and back-rest a single mould of pre-formed plywood was used. To solve the problem of making the head-rest comfortable for everyone who used the chair, a wide slot was cut out and a cushion supported the back of one's neck (Fig 108). The leg structures were made from pre-formed beech laminates, and to avoid using hinges the back-rest panel and front legs formed one assembly and the seat panel and rear legs another. For the chair's six main components – that is, four leg structures, the

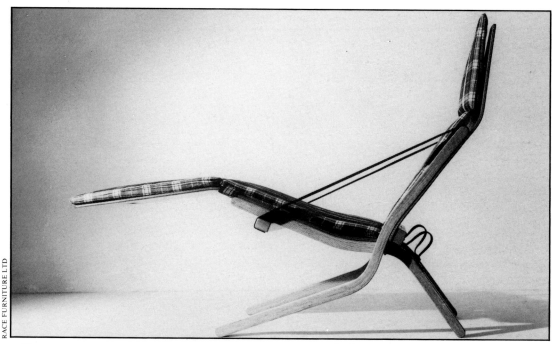

RACE FURNITURE LTD

DESIGN COUNCIL

Fig 104, top: Neptune deck-chair, 1953.
Fig 105, above: Folded prototype Neptune.

seat and the back – only two moulds were needed.[2]

The first group of chairs was put into use, but after a six-month voyage to Australia the adhesive bond of the laminate was failing and the chairs were de-laminating and splitting along the grain of the wood. Also, as a result of chemical action the brass screws were wasting because of de-zincing and the marine varnish had failed. The first step in the re-design programme was to check the adhesive, and tests showed that resorcinol was superior to the urea-formaldehyde used originally.[3] The splitting was initially thought to be caused by failure of the adhesive, but it was found to be related to the choice of laminate. Although gaboon mahogany laminate was as affected by sea conditions as beech, its fibres were closer together and could contain the movement of the

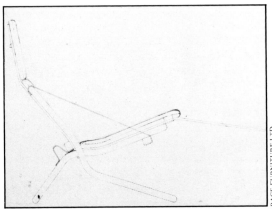

RACE FURNITURE LTD

DESIGN COUNCIL

DESIGN COUNCIL

Fig 106, above left: Sprawler chair of laminated wood 'petals', prototype, 1951.
Fig 107, above: Neptune back and seat profiles.
Fig 108, left: Rear view of Neptune showing head-rest. The back-rest panel and front leg assembly wedged together with the seat panel and rear leg assembly without a hinge, and the load was taken by two straps fastened to the outer end of the leg components. Small woven nylon straps at the back of the chair limited the movement of the sub-assemblies and enabled the chair to fold neatly. The components were held together by brass screws finished with marine varnish.

wood better. It was therefore decided to use this laminate for the Neptune, even though it was not as strong as beech and the components had to be thickened in order to provide the same strength. The problem of the electro-chemical corrosive action on the brass screws was solved by using nylon screw cups to insulate the screw heads from the surrounding wood. This also had the added advantage of making each screw more efficient by increasing its clamping area. After these modifications the Neptune provided reliable service, and from it Race developed the Mermaid which was foldable and stackable (Fig 109).

The experience gained in the design of the Neptune provided the basis for the design of a simpler type of deck chair requested by the Orient Line some six years later. Race's first designs for this were for a folding chair with seat and back made of thin slats of plywood (Fig 110). Subsequently this idea was modified and

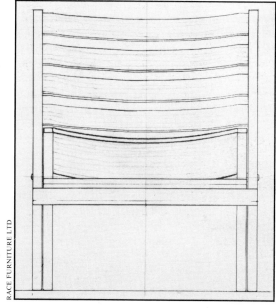

Fig 109, left: Mermaid steamer chair, 1953.
Fig 110, top: Prototype Cormorant showing slats.
Fig 111, above: Cormorant folding outdoor chair, 1959, tropical or sea-going version.

the Cormorant chair (Fig 111) had a single panel seat and back-rest of laminated mahogany, and was intended for use without cushions or upholstery. The leg components were solid afrormosia. Afrormosia had the reputation of rotting and turning black in sea water, but experiments showed that it was not the sea water itself that caused this but sea water in conjunction with metal. Hence, provided the metal hinges of the chair were insulated from the wood with nylon flanged bushes, there should be no trouble. This was found to be the case. The Cormorant was painted with a pigmented epoxy resin finish that proved to give better service than the marine varnish used in the Neptune, although the pigments were not fast to light.[4]

In 1961 the Cormorant won a Design Centre Award and the following year a Gold Medal at the California State Exhibition. In the view of the Design Council judges the chair was comfortable and compact, the method of folding was ingenious and simple and the chair was strong without being clumsy, the natural finish of the timber emphasising the chair's robust appearance.[5] Although it was developed initially as a deck chair for liners, the Cormorant became a popular outdoor chair for domestic use.

During the 1950s the company fulfilled a number of contracts for both deck and indoor furniture for liners. These included the Oriana, Orsova and Canberra of P & O's Orient Line and the Willem Ruys, flagship of the Royal Netherlands Line. One of the design problems posed by P & O's Orient Line was the high cost of renovating upholstered furniture in ships' lounges. Every few months large numbers had to be removed from service because the cushion covers needed cleaning or the arm covers were worn out. The R57 range of chairs and settees was developed to cope with this problem (Fig 112). Traditional loose-covered chairs tended to be of a rather amorphous shape, and

DESIGN COUNCIL

DESIGN COUNCIL

RACE FURNITURE LTD/CARBONORA LTD

Fig 112, opposite: R57 settee and chair with turned beech legs, 1956. A tubular steel sub-frame provided the necessary robustness. The arms and back were of plywood panels covered in plastic foam and upholstered in hide. The seat was of Pirelli webbing, and seat and back cushions were of latex. Zipped cushion covers were removed for cleaning.

Fig 113, top: Tripos E chair, 1959. Square-section steel tube frame in white, grey, cream or graphite. Arms, back and seat frame of oak or mahogany, and cushions with detachable covers.

Fig 114, above: Lecture theatre seating for the University of Liverpool Medical School, 1957.

in the R57 Race was seeking a modern idiom with the convenience for cleaning that loose covers provide. This was achieved by the clarity of form of the chairs, together with the low horizontal emphasis produced by their dimensions. The range consisted of single, two and three seaters.[6]

Contract furniture is not necessarily limited in sale to the company placing the contract and the R57 was sold for hotels, university common rooms and domestic use, as was the Tripos E range, another chair developed at this period for the Orient Line (Fig 113).

An important aspect of the company's contract work was the development of auditorium and lecture theatre seating. The main problem in the design of this type of seating is to devise a basic unit that is flexible enough to fit into a variety of spaces. Each particular situation will vary in the lengths of row required, and the distance between the rows must be carefully controlled, particularly if a writing shelf is fitted to the back of the seat. Furthermore, each location is likely to have a different raking and hence the steps that the seating fits onto will vary.

The first lecture theatre seating developed by Race was for the University of Liverpool Medical School (Fig 114), and consisted of tip-up seating. This design represented Ernest Race's only involvement in this particular area of contract work, but subsequently the design was modified and the company supplied a range of bench and tip-up seating to numerous institutions at home and abroad. In 1965 Peter Dickinson's pedestal auditorium seating designed for Race Furniture Ltd was awarded the Council of Industrial Design's Duke of Edinburgh's Prize for Elegant Design.[7] This type of contract work, if it was to be expanded, demanded space – something that the company was very short of at their Clapham factory.

Sheppey

In 1961 the company changed its name from
Ernest Race Ltd to Race Furniture Ltd and
moved from Clapham in South London to a
new and larger factory at Sheerness on the Isle
of Sheppey.[8] The choice of Sheerness was
dictated primarily by economics; it was a
redevelopment area with high unemployment,
and the financial inducements offered by the
Board of Trade to companies moving there were
very attractive. The site was far away from
traditional furniture making areas and labour
skilled in the techniques of furniture making did
not exist there. Indeed, for the welders,
boilermakers and chippies used to working in
the Naval dockyard, the scale of work
demanded by furniture making was akin to
watchmaking! In addition, many of the skilled
men, such as upholsterers, who had worked for
the company in Clapham decided not to move
with the company. There were virtually no
skilled upholsterers in Sheerness and it was clear
that production had to be revised to suit the new
conditions. Plans for this had been under way
for some time before the move. The first
furniture to be put into production at the new
factory was the Sheppey range in 1961, and this
was followed in 1962 by the Curlew range.

The Sheppey was a development from the
R57 range of chairs designed in 1957 and
supplied to the Orient Line. The prototype
Sheppey, which was developed at Clapham,
used the same basic seat and back frame as the
R57. The thinking behind the development of
the Sheppey range was to produce a standard
set of interchangeable mass-produced
components from which a number of alternative
versions could be assembled. All were based on
a welded steel frame, seats of Pirelli webbing,
fixed back cushions and loose reversible seat
cushions. Two heights of back were offered,
high and low (Fig 115). Alternative end frames

RACE FURNITURE LTD MILLAR & HARRIS

VICTORIA & ALBERT MUSEUM

*Fig 115, top: Sheppey range, 1961. From left:
high-back chair UH 1, chair WL 1 with wooden
end frames, settee ML/2 with metal end frames.
Fig 116, above: Sheppey chair WL/1–3, 1961.
Fig 117, opposite: Detail of Sheppey WL/1–3.*

were available in metal or in various woods. For the wood end-frames local timber of yew, pear and apple was used, each piece individually cut from planks, but when these local supplies came to an end, the company had to offer mahogany, afrormosia and ash.[9] To accompany the chairs two tables were produced, a high table and a coffee table. The top of the high table was level with the top of the arms of the Sheppey settee and chair. The frames of these tables were of square steel tube, stove enamelled in a variety of finishes. The tops were available in mahogany or ash veneers, self-edged Formica or Warerite, or edged with solid wood.

The first Sheppey range to come out of the new factory consisted of 20 pieces of furniture (settees and easy chairs) made up from 13 basic components,[10] though later the range was reduced to 12 different models.[11] All the furniture in the Sheppey range was easily assembled (four nuts and screws for each chair), and all could be packed flat for transport. They were very sturdily constructed and were thus suitable for such contract uses as common rooms or public waiting areas. They were also light enough in appearance to appeal to the retail market.

In 1963 the settee and chair Sheppey WL/1–3

DESIGN COUNCIL

(Fig 116), which had ash ends and fine aluminium strips in the arm joints, were given a Design Centre Award.[12] The points picked out in the award were that they were light, strong and comfortable; they featured a good combination of timber and metal; their proportions were well suited to modern rooms; and their demountable construction made them easily transportable. The award also pinpointed the practical and attractive use of aluminium dowels (Fig 117). These fine aluminium strips at the joints appeared superficially to be inlay; in fact they were the edges of triangular fillets. It was not unusual to use fillets in furniture construction, what was unusual was that a means of providing extra strength could be exploited so successfully to give a decorative effect. The method of production of these end-frames was to machine them as complete units to take the fillets, which were fixed with Araldite. The woodwork was then brushed with melamine lacquer, which was both acid and spirit resistant, then lightly polished.

The pale wood of the Sheppey and the textured upholstery fabric in neutral shades seemed to typify Swedish design. Indeed, in the 1950s and later, 'Swedish modern' became a catch phrase for many of the new ideas in furniture and furnishing. The main characteristics implied by the term were clarity of form with an emphasis on the rectilinear and horizontal, neutral colours and the use of natural materials such as wood, in such a way that their organic nature was appreciated. Wood was not painted or lacquered but clear varnished. The roots of such design lay in both the Modern Movement and the Arts and Crafts Movement, and in the search for a balance between modern technology and the traditional crafts. These sources can be seen in the design and construction of the Sheppey. In the arms the use of wood and metal together draws attention to the grain of the wood and recalls the philosophy of truth to materials so important to the Arts and Crafts Movement.

Demountability and ease of construction were features of the Sheppey and Curlew ranges. The Curlew armless settees and chairs were available with high or low backs and as one, two, three or four seaters. Like the Sheppey they were based on a main frame of welded steel, and the end frames and side rails were of solid mahogany, ash or afrormosia (Fig 118).[13]

The flexibility of the Sheppey and Curlew ranges was appropriate to the longer production runs possible at the new factory. The basic design of each combined attention to detail with a certain anonymity, qualities that tended to be associated with the most successful examples of industrial design. But Race was not an industrial designer, nor did he wish to become one. He was a furniture designer, and by 1960 he had reached the stage in his career where he wanted to expand his range of design rather than concentrate on mass-production. The move of the factory from Clapham to Sheerness, and the future emphasis of the company on longer production runs, brought these feelings to a head. In September 1962 Race resigned from the Board of the company and set up as a consultant designer.

DESIGN COUNCIL SAM LAMBERT

Fig 118: Curlew chair, 1962.

Consultancy

During the late 1950s and early 1960s the furniture industry had undergone some marked changes, with many of the smaller firms going out of business and the medium and larger firms increasing in size. The firms that remained tended to show much more interest in design and consequently there were better opportunities for both the staff designer and the consultant. Some of the most successful results in the area of furniture design had come from designers working as a consultant for a particular company, for example Robert Heritage and Archie Shine; Robin Day and Hille; John and Sylvia Reid and Stag (Fig 119). Consultancy avoided the disadvantages of full-time employment with one firm, which could lead to over-specialisation and staleness, and the disadvantages of the freelance designer, who was faced with isolated commissions and a consequent lack of continuity in the style of a firm's products. Race's career as a consultant designer lasted barely 18 months before he fell ill and died in January 1964. How he might have developed with the broader possibilities available to him is thus open to conjecture, but the few projects that were completed in this brief time give some indication.

One of the first of Race's designs as a consultant was a chair produced by Cintique in 1963[1]. As a consultant designer Race was involved in a number of projects for different companies, but most of them he was unable to complete before he died. The exception to this, apart from Cintique, were designs commissioned by Jack Pritchard for Isokon Furniture Co: the Isokon Penguin Donkey bookcase Mark 2 and the Isokon Bottleship. The original Donkey and Bottleship dated from 1939 and were designed by Egon Riss and Jack Pritchard (Figs 120 and 121). Race had known Pritchard through the Furniture Development Council and from Pritchard's Lawn Road Flats

days before the war.

Isokon was originally set up by Pritchard in 1931 with the aim of applying modern functional design to houses, flats, furniture and fittings. Pritchard was very interested in the Modern Movement and while he was working for Venesta Plywood Co in Paris in 1922–30 he saw some of Le Corbusier's work. He also visited Stuttgart with the architect Wells Coates and saw the houses built by Mies van der Rohe, Gropius, Le Corbusier and others for the Weissenhof Exhibition in 1927, went to the Bauhaus in Dessau and met Erich Mendelssohn in Berlin. Lawn Road Flats, Hampstead (1934), designed by Wells Coates for Isokon, can be seen very much as the response by Pritchard and Wells Coates to the stimulus provided by the Continental pioneers.[2] The international character of Lawn Road Flats was not restricted to its architecture and design, for many refugees from Nazi Germany came to live there. These for a while included Gropius, Breuer and Moholy-Nagy.

In 1935 Pritchard left Venesta, although he was retained as a consultant, and set up Isokon Furniture Co;[3] Gropius was the first controller of design. The principal material to be used in the designs for the company was plywood and '. . . the furniture will be primarily useful and its aesthetic qualities will be due to its form rather than superimposed ornament'.[4] Isokon had sold plywood furniture from other companies such as The Makers of Simple Furniture, and Pritchard himself had designed furniture in plywood. For the new company both Gropius and Breuer put forward designs and among the most successful items were Breuer's long chair and nesting tables (Fig 122).

The designs by Egon Riss and Pritchard for the Penguin Donkey and the Bottleship were made of very thin plywood with flowing curves. However, their proposed production virtually

Fig 120: Penguin Donkey, Jack Pritchard and Egon Riss, 1939 (Isokon).

Fig 119, top: Bedroom furniture, John and Sylvia Reid, 1960 (The Stag Cabinet Co).
Fig 121, above: Bottleship, Jack Pritchard and Egon Riss, 1939 (Isokon).

LONG CHAIR
price from £6.15.0
upholstered in your fabric

SHORT CHAIR
price from £5.15.0
upholstered in your fabric

STOOL
price from 6.6

TRAY
price 8.

TABLE (Stool + Tray)
price from 14.6

NEST OF TABLES
price £3.13.6

OCCASIONAL TABLE
price from £1.5.0

FURNITURE CREATED FOR AN AGE OF EASE

ISOKON furniture has been designed by some of the leading European designers, such well-known artists as Professor Walter Gropius, Marcel Breuer (who created the long and short ISOKON chairs), Christopher Nicholson and R. D. Russell. New ideas are constantly being tested. If you care to send us a card, we will tell you where to find your nearest ISOKON stockist and will keep you in touch with future developments.

THE ISOKON FURNITURE COMPANY

ISOKON ISOKON FLATS · LAWN ROAD · LONDON · NW3

TELEPHONE PRIMROSE 6054

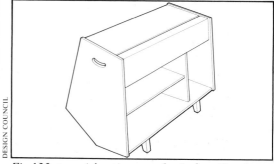

Fig 122, top: Advertisement for Isokon Furniture Company from a MARS exhibition, 1938.
Fig 123, left: Penguin Donkey Mark 2, 1963 (Isokon).
Fig 124, above: Bottleship, 1963 (Isokon).

coincided with the outbreak of the Second World War, when the supply of plywood from Estonia and Finland was cut off, so Isokon Furniture Co had to cease production. After the war Pritchard made several attempts to revive the company, but it was not until 1963 when he retired from the post of Director of the Furniture Development Council that he was in a position to do so.

When Pritchard commissioned Race to undertake new designs, the thin plywood that had been used for the originals was no longer available. Race's designs used thicker plywood. Also, unlike the originals, Race's designs were of a knock-down construction that could be packed flat and posted (Fig 123).[5] The Donkey Mark 2 was designed to hold about 90 Penguin books with space between the two sides for newspapers and magazines. Assembly involved eight screws, and a screwdriver was supplied. It was produced by John Alan Designs until 1980.

The Bottleship (Fig 124) was about 17in (43.2cm) high and was designed to take six full-sized bottles and glasses. The lid opened to form a bar top and there was a rack on one side to hold magazines and newspapers.

At Race Furniture Ltd Race's opportunity for working in plywood had been limited to the Neptune, Mermaid and Cormorant deck-chairs and the earlier prototype easy chair, the Sprawler. Isokon gave him the opportunity to start designing again in this material, and had he been able to continue, 'he might have done as good work in plywood as Alvar Aalto'.[6]

Throughout Race's career his designs illustrated his concern to develop his ideas for using particular materials, the only exception to this being the early aluminium furniture. One idea led logically to the next, and he was far more concerned to exploit the potential of a particular medium as far as possible and to produce something good than to produce something new and fashionable. 'The one thing we must guard against is the desire for the new rather than the good, for the fashionable rather than the well designed.'[7] He tended to be a man of few words, not given to making pronouncements on his philosophy of design, preferring that his work should stand as the example; although when he did express his views on such matters as the role of ergonomics in design, he did so succinctly. The scientific approach to design, and the role that ergonomics and anthropometrics could play, were recognised by Race as useful in increasing the area of measured knowledge available to a designer. However, such techniques could not design a chair, only a designer could do that. Race confessed to some irritation 'when words such as anthropometrics and ergonomics are bandied about with the implied suggestion that any moment now the Scientist with a capital S will have cleared the jungle in which designers have been endlessly thrashing about for years!'[8]

Race was involved in the education of designers, serving on various committees, on the boards of governors of art schools, and acting as Visitor or External Assessor for furniture design courses. He advised aspiring furniture designers that they should have an absorbing interest in the construction, shape and purpose of things in general and of furniture in particular, otherwise the profession was not for them.[9] Furthermore, he thought they should avoid over-specialisation in the early stages. The new diploma courses in design[10] provided a broader and more liberal education which he thought would produce the sort of designers that industry needed.

The two highest awards available to a designer in the UK are election to the Royal Society of Arts, Faculty of Royal Designers for Industry, which Race achieved in 1953, and the

Society of Industrial Artists and Designers' Design Medal. This Race was awarded in 1963 and the citation pinpointed his originality, his ability to see the potential for new manufacturing methods and the simplicity of his designs in terms of both production and use. The rather nationalistic flavour of the citation – 'The complete originality of his work could claim to be genuinely indigenous to this country: there was nothing pseudo-Scandinavian about it'[11] – raises the question of the influences on Race during the course of his career.

Some critics[12] have been keen to cite Eames as an important influence, and certainly Race admired his work, but disputed that he was one of the major influences on him.[13] Race admired the craftsmanship of much of the work from Finland, Denmark and Sweden and saw the Finns as leaders in world design,[14] but he felt the vogue, in the late 1950s and early 1960s, for beautifully finished teak furniture was a yearning for the past, and that there was something not quite right in the modern world in its emphasis on hand-finished natural materials. The challenge of the possibilities of man-made materials was an exciting one that would have to be faced.

The question of the major influences on Race can only be approached by looking at specific designs and the context in which they were produced. Race was a designer, and designers are interested in the world about them: new materials, new techniques, the work of contemporaries, the work of the past are all part of that world and are likely to have some influence, though the form these influences take are often difficult, if not impossible, to determine.

Throughout Race's career the dominant criteria applied to design were those of the Modern Movement. Only in the early 1960s did those criteria become increasingly questioned under the onslaught of pop design, and never again would views of what was good design and what was not be as clear as they were to the adherents of the Modern Movement.

In any period attitudes towards design – whether of the present or of the past – are influenced by the intellectual and stylistic criteria of the time. In the 1950s, under the influence of the Modern Movement, everything Victorian and Edwardian was still regarded as tasteless. Houses were stripped of their plastering, doors and staircases were flush-panelled and fireplaces were ripped out. Today great effort and expense are involved in restoring these houses to their original state.

Today's criteria for assessing design are influenced by many factors. These include a reaction against the Modern Movement, the influence of pop design and the craft revival of the 1970s, and the development of alternative design. The influence of pop design can be seen in the emphasis on bright colours and surface decoration, while the craft revival has stimulated an interest in natural materials and organic forms, seen particularly well in ceramics. This and the concern for the use of the earth's resources and for ecological balance formed part of the reaction against industrialisation and a consumer oriented society.

Design and fashion are not synonymous, and any assessment of a designer's contribution must seek to take present criteria into account. Design in the 1950s – and this includes much of Race's work – is still regarded as peculiar, if it is not actively disliked. Little move to collect examples of 'contemporary' design is detectable and the 1950s are still out of fashion. The aim of this study has been to try to counter questions of taste and fashion by looking at the contexts in which Race's designs evolved, for it is only by understanding these that one can gain some insight into the problems faced by the designer.

The design of the BA range of furniture was dictated by the lack of traditional furniture-making materials and the demands of the Utility Furniture Scheme. Race's skill as a designer lay in the use he made of the only materials available to him and the ingenuity with which he used those materials. The Festival of Britain was intended to be fun, a 'tonic', and the reason why so many people identified with Race's furniture at the South Bank was that its wit and lightness encapsulated those feelings. Questions as to whether the furniture was 'modern' in the Modern Movement sense were in that context irrelevant, a fact no doubt recognised by the selectors in making their choice of Race's designs. Yet the links between 'contemporary' design and the Modern Movement are strong, although visually this is not immediately apparent. Both sought simplicity, honest expression in the use of materials and economic solutions to a problem, and neither used ornament. It is in the vocabulary of forms used to express these ideas that the major difference lies: the Modern Movement with its emphasis on geometric forms, 'contemporary' with its emphasis on organic forms.

All of Race's designs for Ernest Race Ltd and Race Furniture Ltd were evolved within a very controlled budget. The company was never wealthy nor in a position to invest in the major new tooling that manufacture in plastics would have necessitated. Experimental work was undertaken, as in the development work for the Neptune, but financially the scope within the company for this was limited. The problem of working within a very restricted budget is one of the many challenges that a designer must meet, and Race was well aware of its importance. Despite the restrictions imposed by a tight budget, he nevertheless produced furniture that is still a pleasure to live with, and the Neptune, the early rocking chair, the Heron, Flamingo and Sheppey chairs, and the Antelope and Springbok still grace many homes.

Notes and References

Ernest Race and Ernest Race Ltd

1　First year students, whether studying interior design or architecture, took the same course, learning the orders of architecture and producing a fully rendered drawing.

2　A.B. Read RDI was in charge of design at the time.

3　Geoffrey Dunn recalled selling some of Race's Indian fabrics in his shop. (Interview, 11 October 1979.)

4　Interview, Sally Race, 9 March 1979.

5　Letter, E. Race to J. Pritchard, Furniture Development Council, 12 January 1963.

6　Race, E. Introduction to *Scandinavian Domestic Design*, E. Zahle (ed), Methuen, 1963.

7　Race, E. 'The Furniture Designer-Manufacturer', *SIAJ*, no 96, February 1961, pp4–5.

8　Race, E. 'Professional Practice, Product Design, Machine Based'. Draft of paper presented to Conference on Professional Practice, undated.

9　Interview, Sally Race, 9 March 1979.

10　Illustration no 1 in *Design*, no 184, April 1964, p55 is captioned 'prototype . . . designed 1945 but never produced'. An identical photograph appeared in *Ideal Home*, January 1947, and a variation using the same units in a slightly differing configuration. It would appear that this photograph relates to a later design. (See Fig 33.)

11　Noel Jordan, J.W. Draft of article for Heal's House Magazine dated 14 March 1973.

12　Letter, Noel Jordan to Race, 14 August 1945.

13　*Ibid*.

14　Directors of the Company were J.W. Noel Jordan 45 per cent, Ernest Race 35 per cent and H.O. Hayward 20 per cent. Hayward was Director-Secretary.

15　Letter, Noel Jordan to Race, 25 October 1945.

The Utility Furniture Scheme

1　Geffrye Museum, *Utility Furniture and Fashion 1941–51*, Catalogue, ILEA, London, 1974.

2　Russell, G. *Designer's Trade*, Allen and Unwin, London, 1968.

3　Board of Trade, Working Party Report, *Furniture*, HMSO, London, 1946.

4　Douglas, W.S. *Report of the Purchase Tax/Utility Committee*, HMSO, London, 1952.

5　*Ibid*, p9.

6　It is tempting to assume that, because these chairs were made from aluminium, the initials stood for something such as 'British Aluminium'. However, this was not the case. Race's furniture using aluminium included the BB range of coffee tables, BC range of lounge and dining tables, a BD 1 sideboard cabinet, CB range of bookcases, BC range of desks, a telephone cabinet AA 1, and the DA range of easy chairs and settee.

7　Letter, J.F. Sloan & Sons, Enniskillen, to Race Furniture Ltd, 3 July 1963. The BA 3A had arms.

The BA Chair and Metal Furniture

1　For equivalent volumes, steel weighs approximately three times as much as aluminium.

2　For further reading see H.L.C. Jaffe, *de Stijl*, London, 1970; S. Starr, *Russian Modernism: Culture and the Avant-Garde 1900–1930*, 1976; J. Golding and C. Green, *Leger and Purist Paris*, Tate Gallery Exhibition Catalogue, 1970; Le Corbusier, *Towards a New Architecture*, London, 1974.

3　Le Corbusier used bentwood chairs in his Pavillon de L'Esprit Nouveau in 1925.

4　The weight of the alloy was 10lb 2oz (5.1kg); the 12 bolts would have collectively supported 12 tons (12.19 tonnes)! Subsequently $\frac{1}{4}$in (6.3mm) diameter screws were used.

5   Interview, Leslie Smith, 9 November 1979. Now Design and Development Manager for Race Furniture Ltd, Leslie Smith joined Ernest Race Ltd as an apprentice in 1951.
6   Race Furniture Ltd, *Race,* Submission to Royal Society of Arts for Design Management Award, 1969.
7   Noel Jordan, J.W. Draft of article, *op cit.*
8   Ernest Race Ltd, Catalogue, 1946/7.
9   *Ibid.*
10 Interview, Leslie Smith, 9 November 1979.
11 *Ibid.*
12 Council of Industrial Design, Minutes, 13 September 1946.
13 Interview, Geoffrey Dunn, 11 October 1979.

The Festival Chairs and Contemporary Design
1   Whitechapel Art Gallery, *Setting up Home,* Catalogue, 1952.
2   OECD Main Economic Indicators, June 1968.
3   *Festival of Britain,* Catalogue of Exhibits, HMSO, London, 1951, p12.
4   *Ibid,* p13.
5   Interview, Sir Gordon Russell, 26 April 1979.
6   Race, E. 'Talking Design', *The Formica Journal,* vol 4, no 4, April-May 1960, pp14–16.
7   *Ibid.*
8   Interview, Sir Gordon Russell, 26 April 1979.
9   Interview, Leslie Smith, 9 November 1979.
10 No documentary evidence for this has been found, nor was it confirmed by Sir Gordon Russell when interviewed.
11 Banham, M. and Hillier, B. (eds) *A Tonic to the Nation,* London, 1976, p190.
12 Antelopes with white plastic ferrules appear for the first time in the catalogue for January 1958.
13 The original Antelope table was square with legs and ball feet stove-enamelled white, cream/grey or graphite. Plates were welded over the top of the legs to screw to the top of $\frac{3}{4}$in (1.89cm) plywood. In 1956 a new design was introduced which was circular and very similar to the Gazelle table (Fig 98), but with three legs, not four; this design was also called Antelope.
14 Ernest Race Ltd, Catalogue, 1952.
15 This design was welcomed by the National Spastics Society, according to information put out by the company.

Steel Rod Furniture
1   Interview, Sir Gordon Russell, 26 April 1979.
2   Noel Jordan, J.W. Draft of article, *op cit.*
3   All items qualified as Utility.
4   Sheridan, M. (ed) *The Furnisher's Encyclopedia,* London, 2nd ed, 1955, p100.
5   Interview, Leslie Smith, 9 November 1979.
6   *Ibid.*
7   *Ibid.*
8   *Design,* no 126, June 1959, p35.
9   Interview, Sally Race, 9 March 1979.
10 McCallum, I. 'Prestige and Utility. Time Life's London Offices', *Architectural Review,* vol 115, March 1953, p157.
11 Interview, Leslie Smith, 9 November 1979.
12 The Gazelle table appears in the Race catalogue for January 1958. It does not appear in the 1951 or 1953 catalogues studied by the author, yet this table appears identical to those in Figure 42.

Contract Furniture
1   Letter, Adrian Heath, 30 October 1979.
2   Race Furniture Ltd, *Race, op cit,* p9.
3   *Ibid,* p10 for full details of these tests.
4   Noel Jordan's concern for detail is illustrated by the fact that the Cormorant had 23 screws and all their slots had to be aligned! (Interview, Leslie Smith.)
5   *Design,* no 150, June 1961, p56.
6   Ernest Race Ltd, Catalogue, 1957.
7   Peter Dickinson joined the company in 1957 and became chief designer after Race left the company in 1962.

8 Officially opened on 30 March 1962 by the Director of the Council of Industrial Design, Sir Paul Reilly (now Lord Reilly).

9 Interview, Leslie Smith, 9 November 1979.

10 *Design,* no 159, March 1962, p53.

11 Race Furniture Ltd, Catalogue, 1967.

12 *Design,* no 174, June 1963, pp48–9.

13 Race Furniture Ltd, Catalogue, 1967.

Consultancy

1 All details of this design were subsequently destroyed in a fire. The only photograph discovered so far appeared in *Design,* no 184, April 1964, p55.

2 For further details see Cantacuzino, S. *Wells Coates,* London, 1978, ch 3.

3 A new company, distinct from the original Isokon set up in 1931.

4 Jack Pritchard Archive, School of Architecture, University of Newcastle-upon-Tyne. Quoted in Grieve, A. 'Isokon', *Hampstead in the Thirties,* Catalogue, 1974–5, p11.

5 Isokon Furniture Ltd, *News from Isokon,* 13 April 1964.

6 Interview, Sir Gordon Russell, 26 April 1979.

7 Race, E. 'Talking Design', *The Formica Journal, op cit.*

8 Letter, Race to J. Pritchard, Furniture Development Council, 9 January 1963.

9 Race, E. 'Furniture Design', *SIAJ,* no 4, June 1948, p5.

10 National Council for Diplomas in Art and Design, set up to administer the award of diplomas in 1961.

11 1963 Design Medal Citation, *SIAJ,* June 1963, p47.

12 Banham, M. and Hillier, B. (eds) *op cit,* p190.

13 Letter, Race to J. Pritchard, Furniture Development Council, 12 June 1963.

14 *Design,* no 169, January 1963, p57.

Further Reading

Aloi, R. *Esempi di Arredamento di Tutto il Mondo*, Hoepli, Milan, 1950.

Aloi, R. *Sedie, Poltroni, Divani*, Hoepli, Milan, 1953 and 1957.

Arts Council of Great Britain. *Thirties: British Art and Design before the War*, Catalogue, London, 1980.

Banham, M. and Hillier, B. (eds) *A Tonic to the Nation: The Festival of Britain 1951*, Thames and Hudson, London, 1976.

Board of Trade. *Working Party Report on Furniture*, HMSO, London, 1946.

Board of Trade. *Report of the Gorell Committee on the Production and Exhibition of Articles of Good Design and Everyday Use*, HMSO, London, 1932.

Bonnard, J.R. *La Système Utility*, Paris, 1953.

Bonnet, D. (ed) *Contemporary Cabinet Design and Construction*, London, 1956.

Camden Arts Centre. *Hampstead in the Thirties Exhibition*, Catalogue, London, 1975.

Camden Arts Centre. *Classics of Modern Design Exhibition*, Catalogue, London, 1977.

Carrington, N. *Design and Decoration in the Home*, Country Life, London, 1952.

Council for Art and Industry. *The Working Class Home: Its Furnishing and Equipment*, HMSO, London, 1957.

Council of Industrial Design. *Britain Can Make It Exhibition*, Catalogue, HMSO, London, 1946.

Douglas, W.S. *Report of the Purchase Tax/Utility Committee*, HMSO, London, 1952.

Drexler, A. *Charles Eames: Furniture from the Design Collection*, Museum of Modern Art, New York, 1973.

Farr, M. *Design in British Industry: a Mid-Century Survey*, Cambridge University Press, 1953.

Festival of Britain, Catalogue of Exhibits, HMSO, London, 1951.

Festival of Britain, South Bank Exhibition Guide, HMSO, London, 1951.

Frederick S. Wight Art Gallery. *Connections: The Work of Charles and Ray Eames*, University of California, 1977.

Geffrye Museum. *Utility Furniture and Fashion 1941–51 Exhibition*, Catalogue, ILEA, London, 1974.

Gloag, J. (ed) *Design in Modern Life*, Allen and Unwin, London, 1934.

Goldfinger, E. *British Furniture Today*, Tiranti, London, 1951.

Halsey, A.H. (ed) *Trends in British Society since 1900: a Guide to the Changing Social Structure of Britain*, Macmillan, London, 1963.

Hård af Segerstad, U. *Modern Scandinavian Furniture*, Studio, London, 1963. (Translated by N. and E. Maze).

Hatje, G. (ed) *International Design Annual*, Verlag Hatje, Stuttgart, 1952.

Hurstfield, J. *History of the Second World War: The Control of Raw Materials*, HMSO, London, 1953.

Joel, D. *The Adventure of British Furniture*, Ernest Benn, London, 1953.

Johnson, P. *Machine Art Exhibition*, Catalogue, Museum of Modern Art, New York, 1934.

Kaufmann, E. Jr. *Prize Designs for Modern Furniture from the International Competition for Low Cost Furniture Design*, Museum of Modern Art, New York, 1950.

Lewis, F. *British Designers, their Work*, F. Lewis, Leigh on Sea, 1942.

Logie, G. *Furniture from Machines*, Allen and Unwin, London, 1947.

Meigge, R. *Home Timber Production 1939–45*, Lockwood, London, 1949.

Noyes, E.F. *Organic Design in Home Furnishing*, Museum of Modern Art, New York, 1941.

Pevsner, N. *An Enquiry into Industrial Art in England*, Cambridge University Press, 1937.

Pleydell-Bouverie, M. *Daily Mail Book of Post War Houses*, Daily Mail, London, 1944.

Russell, G. *Designer's Trade*, Allen and Unwin, London, 1968.

Ruusuvuori, A. (ed) *Alvar Aalto 1898–1976 Exhibition*, Catalogue, Museum of Finnish Architecture, 1978.

Sharp, D., Benton, T. and Campbell Cole, B. *PEL and Tubular Steel Furniture of the Thirties*, Architectural Association, London, 1977.